Military Ribbon Guide
Army, Marine Corps, Navy, Air Force, Space Force & Coast Guard

How To Use This Book

Welcome to Medals of America's military ribbons book covering all five armed forces military ribbons. This book covers all military awards since the Civil War and shows each branch ribbon chests from World War II, Korea, Vietnam, the Cold War, the Liberation of Kuwait, NATO actions, Iraq, Afghanistan and Syria. The ribbons of the Army, Navy, Marine Corps, Air Force, Space Force and Coast Guard are displayed in correct order of wear with all of their possible attachments shown below each ribbon. For example, an active duty soldier or veteran can view the the Army pages and identify their ribbons in the correct order of precedence. You can go to the facing page for your last or current branch and see the correct order for multiple service awards. For additional information or to order full sized medals, ribbons or skill and qualification badges go to **www.usmedals.com**.

www.moapress.com

Published by:
Medals of America Press
114 Southchase Blvd.
Fountain Inn, SC 29644

ISBN - 978-1-884452-65-9 (eBook)
ISBN - 978-1-884452-64-2 (Softrback)

Copyright © 2025 by Medals of America Press.

All rights reserved. No part of this publication may be reproduced, stored in a retrieval system or transmitted by any means, electronic, mechanical or by photocopying without written permission from the publishers.

A History of United States Armed Forces Decorations, Unit Awards & Service Ribbons

Medal of Honor	Medal of Honor Civil War	Medal of Honor Army-1896	Medal of Honor (Original Width)	Marine Corps Brevet Medal	Distinguished Service Cross	Distinguished Service Cross ("French Cut")	Navy Cross	Navy Cross (1st Ribbon)
Air Force Cross	Coast Guard Cross	Certificate of Merit (Obsolete)	Defense Distinguished Service Medal	Army Distinguished Service Medal	Army Disting. Service Medal ("French Cut")	Navy Distinguished Service Medal	Navy Dist. Service Medal (1st Ribbon)	Air Force Distinguished Service Medal
Homeland Security Dist. Service Medal	Transportation Dist. Service Medal (Obsolete)	Coast Guard Distinguished Service Medal	Silver Star	D.O.T. Secty's Outstanding Achievm't Medal (Obsolete)	Defense Superior Service Medal	DOT Guardian Medal (USCG) (Obsolete)	Legion of Merit (Chief Commander)	Legion of Merit (Commander)
Legion of Merit (Officer)	Legion of Merit (Legionnaire)	Legion of Merit (Neck Ribbon)	Distinguished Flying Cross	Soldier's Medal	Navy and Marine Corps Medal	Airman's Medal	Coast Guard Medal	Coast Guard Medal (Proposed)
Bronze Star Medal	Purple Heart	Defense Meritorious Service Medal	Meritorious Service Medal	Air Medal	Aerial Achievement Medal	D.O.T. Meritorious Achvm't Medal (Obsolete)	Joint Service Commendation Medal	Army Commendation Medal
Navy & Marine Corps Commendation Medal	Air Force Commendation Medal	Coast Guard Commendation Medal	D.O.T. Secy's Superior Achievement (Obsolete)	Joint Service Achievement Medal	Army Achievement Medal	Navy & USMC Achievement Medal	Air & Space Achievement Medal	DOT 9-11 Medal (USCG) (Obsolete)
Coast Guard Achievement Medal	USCG Commandant's Letter of Commendation	Navy & Marine Corps Combat Action Ribbon	Air Force Combat Action Medal	Coast Guard Combat Action Ribbon	Wound Ribbon (1917) (Never Issued)	Army Presidential Unit Citation	Navy Presidential Unit Citation	Air Force Presidential Unit Citation
Coast Guard Presidential Unit Citation	Joint Meritorious Unit Award	Army Valorous Unit Award	Navy Unit Commendation	Air Force Gallant Unit Citation	D.O.T. Secy's Outst. Unit Award (Obsolete)	Coast Guard Unit Commendation	Army Meritorious Unit Commendation	Navy Meritorious Unit Commendation
Air Force Meritorious Unit Award	Coast Guard Meritorious Unit Commendation	Army Superior Unit Award	Air Force Outstanding Unit Award	Coast Guard Meritorious Team Comndatn	Navy "E" Ribbon	Air Force Organizational Excellence Award	Coast Guard "E" Ribbon	Coast Guard Bicentenniel Unit Commendation
Gold Lifesaving Medal	Silver Lifesaving Medal	Prisoner of War Medal	Air Force Combat Readiness Medal	Army Good Conduct Medal	Reserve Special Comm. Ribbon (Obsolete)	Navy Good Conduct Medal	Navy Good Conduct Medal (2nd Ribbon)	Navy Good Conduct Medal (1st Ribbon)
Navy Good Conduct Badge (1869-84)	Marine Corps Good Conduct Medal	Marine Good Conduct Medal (1st Ribbon)	Air Force Good Conduct Medal	Coast Guard Good Conduct Medal	U.S.C.G. Good Conduct Medal (1st Ribbon)	Army Reserve Components Achvm't Medal	Naval Reserve Merit. Svs Medal (Obsolete)	Selected Marine Corps Reserve Medal
Fleet Marine Force Reserve Medal- (Obs.)	Air Reserve Forces Meritor's Service Medal	Coast Guard Reserve Good Conduct Medal	Coast Guard Enlisted Person of the Year	Navy Fleet Marine Force Rib. (Obsolete)	Outstanding Airman of the Year Ribbon	Air Force Recognition Ribbon	Civil War Campaign Medal (1861-65)	Civil War Campaign (1st Army Ribbon)
Indian Campaign Medal (1865-91)	Indian Campaign Medal (1st Ribbon)	Dewey Medal (1898)	Sampson Medal (1898)	Spanish Campaign Medal (1898)	Spanish Campaign Medal (1st Army Ribbon)	Spanish Campaign Medal (1st Navy Ribbon)	Cardenas Medal of Honor (1898)	Specially Meritorious Medal (1898)
West Indies Campaign Medal (1898)	West Indies Campaign (1st Ribbon)	Spanish War Service Medal (1898)	Cuban Occupation Medal (1898-1902)	Puerto Rican Occupation Medal (1898)	Philippine Campaign Medal (1899 - 1913)	Philippine Campaign (1st Navy Ribbon)	Philippine Congressional Medal (1899-1902)	China Campaign Medal (1900-01)

Military Ribbon Guide

A History of United States Armed Forces Decorations, Unit Awards & Service Ribbons

China Relief Expedition (1st Navy Ribbon)	Cuban Pacification Medal (1906-09)	Peary Polar Expedit'n Medal (1908-09)	Mexican Service Medal (1911-17)	1st Nicaraguan Campaign Medal (1912)	Haitian Campaign Medal (1915)	Dominican Campaign Medal (1916)	Mexican Border Service Medal (1916-17)	World War I Victory Medal (1917 - 18)
Texas Cavalry Congressional Medal (1918)	Occupation of Germany (1918-23)	N.C.-4 Medal (1919)	Haitian Campaign Medal (1919-20)	2nd Nicaraguan Camp'n Medal (1926-33)	Yangtze Service Medal (1926-32)	1st Byrd Antarctic Expedit'n (1928-30)	Navy Expeditionary Medal	Marine Corps Expeditionary Medal
2nd Byrd Antarctic Expedit'n (1933-35)	China Service Medal (1937, 1945)	Amer. Defense Service Medal (1939-41)	Women's Army Corps Service Medal	American Campaign Medal (1941-46)	Asiatic-Pacific Camp'n Medal (1941-46)	Europe-African-Mid East Camp'gn (1941-46)	World War II Victory Medal (1941 - 46)	U.S. Antarctic Expedit'n Medal (1939-41)
World War II Occupat'n Medal (1945-57)	Medal for Humane Action (1948-49)	Nat'l Defense Service Medal 50,61,90,01,23	Korean Service Medal (1950-54)	Antarctica Service Medal	Coast Guard Arctic Service Medal	Armed Forces Expeditionary Medal	Vietnam Service Medal (1965-73)	Southwest Asia Service Medal (1991-95)
Kosovo Campaign Medal (1999-2013)	Afghanistan Campaign Medal (2001 - 2021)	Iraq Campaign Medal (2003 - 2011)	Inherent Resolve Campaign Medal (2014-)	War on Terrorism Expeditionary Medal (2001-)	War on Terrorism Service Medal (2001- 2022)	Korea Defense Service Medal (1954-)	Armed Forces Service Medal	Humanitarian Service Medal
Mil. Outstanding Volunteer Service Medal	Army Sea Duty Ribbon	Armed Forces Reserve Medal	Army NCO Prof. Development Ribbon	Army Service Ribbon	Army Overseas Service Ribbon	Army Reserve Comp. Overseas Training Ribbon	Navy Sea Service Deployment Ribbon	Navy Arctic Service Medal
Naval Reserve Sea Service Ribbon	Navy & Marine Corps Overseas Service Ribbon	Navy Recruiting Service Ribbon	Navy Acession Training Service Ribbon	Navy Ceremonial Duty Ribbon	Navy Basic Military Tng Honor Graduate Ribbon	Naval Reserve Medal (Obsolete)	Marine Corps Recruiting Ribbon	Marine Corps Drill Instructor Ribbon
Marine Corps Security Guard Ribbon	Marine Corps Combat Instructor Ribbon	Marine Corps Reserve Ribbon (Obsolete)	Remote Combat Effects Medal	Air & Space Campaign Medal	USAF Nuclear Deterrence Opns Medal	Air Force Overseas Ribbon (Short Tour)	Air Force Overseas Ribbon (Long Tour)	Air Force Expeditionary Service Ribbon
Air Force Longevity Service Award	Air Force Special Duty Ribbon	Air Force Miltry Trnng Instructor Rib'n (Obsolete)	Air Force Recruiter Ribbon (Obsolete)	Air Force NCO Prof. Military Education Grad.	Air Force Basic Military Training Honor Graduate	Air Force Small Arms Expert Marksman	Air Force Training Ribbon	Transprttn 9-11 Ribbon (Coast Guard) (Obsolete)
Coast Guard Special Oper'ns Service Ribbon	Coast Guard Sea Service Ribbon	Coast Guard Restricted Duty Ribbon	Coast Guard Overseas Service Ribbon	Coast Guard Basic Training Honor Graduate Ribbon	Coast Guard Recruiting Service Ribbon	Philippine Presidential Unit Citation	Korean Presidential Unit Citation	Vietnam Presidential Unit Citation
Vietnam Gallantry Cross Unit Citation	Philippine Defense Medal	Philippine Liberation Medal (1944 - 45)	Philippine Independence Medal (1946)	United Nations Korean Service Medal	UN Palestine Mission (UNTSO)	UN India/ Pakistan Mission (UNMOGIP)	UN New Guinea Mission (UNTEA)	UN Iraq/ Kuwait Mission (UNIKOM)
UN Western Sahara Mission (MINURSO)	UN Cambodia Mission 1 (UNAMIC)	UN Yugoslavia Mission (UNPROFOR)	UN Cambodia Mission 2 (UNTAC)	UN Somalia Mission (UNOSOM)	UN Haiti Mission (UNMIH)	UN Special Service Medal (UNSSM)	NATO Medal for Bosnia	NATO Medal for Kosovo
NATO Medal for Operation Eagle Assist	NATO Medal for Operation Active Endeavor	NATO Medal for Balkan Operations	NATO Medal for Afghanistan, Sudan, Iraq	Multinational Force & Observers Medal	Inter-American Defense Board Medal	Republic of Vietnam Campaign Medal	Kuwait Liberation Medal (Saudi Arabia)	Kuwait Liberation Medal (Kuwait)
Republic of Korea War Service Medal	Navy Distinguished Marksman Badge	Navy Distinguished Pistol Shot Badge	Navy Dist. Marksman & Pistol Shot	Navy Rifle Marksmanship Ribbon	Navy Pistol Marksmanship Ribbon	Coast Guard Dist. Marksman & Pistol Shot	Coast Guard Rifle Marksmanship Ribbon	Coast Guard Pistol Marksmanship Ribbon

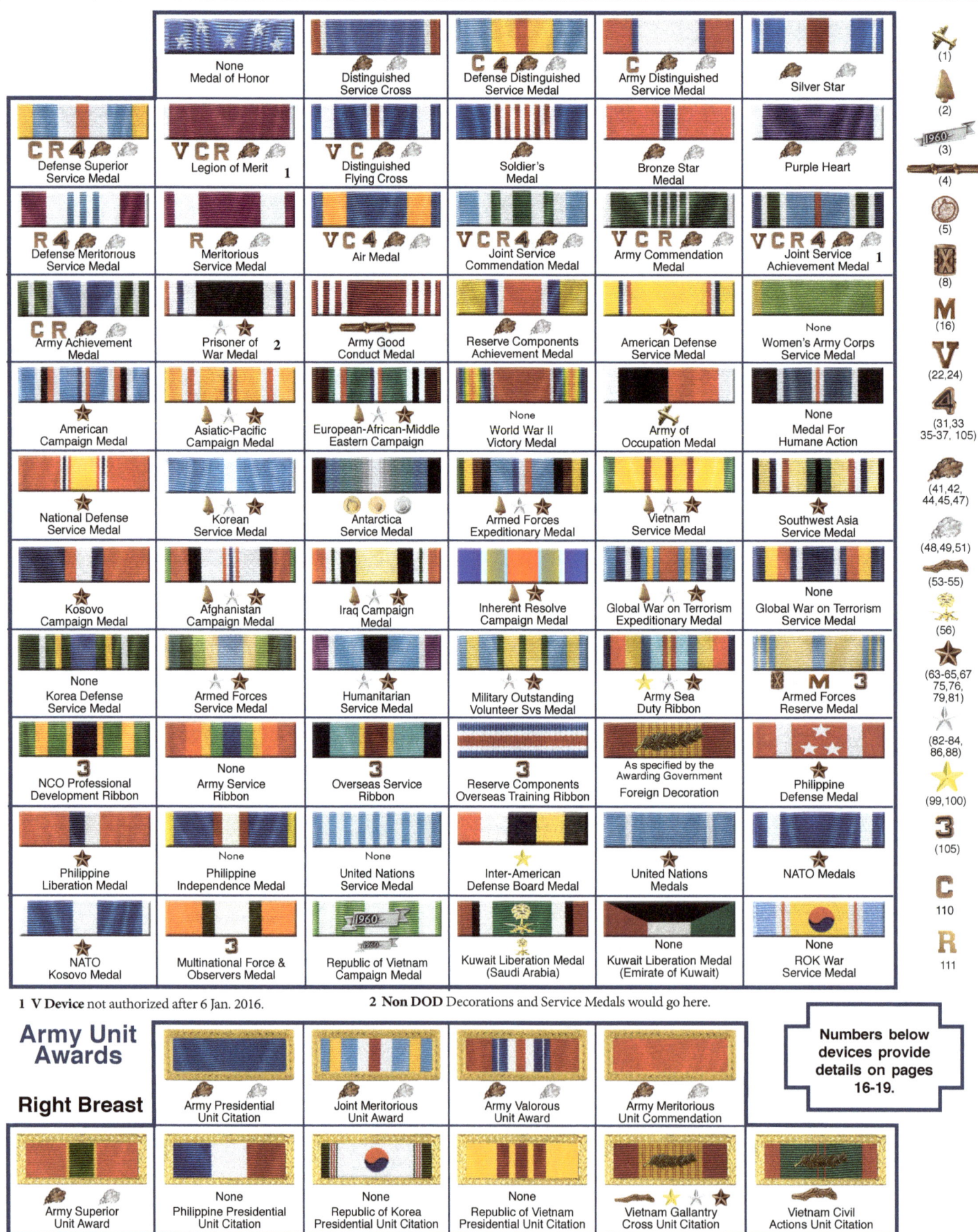

Correct Wear of Multi-Service Awards on the Uniform

Army Order of Precedence *(Other Services in Italics)*

Medal of Honor (Army, Navy, Air Force)
Distinguished Service Cross
Navy Cross
Air Force Cross
Coast Guard Cross
Defense Distinguished Service Medal
Army Distinguished Service Medal
Navy Distinguished Service Medal
Air Force Distinguished Service Medal
Homeland Security Dist. Service Medal
Transportation Dist. Service Medal
Coast Guard Distinguished Service Medal
Silver Star
Defense Superior Service Medal
Legion of Merit
Distinguished Flying Cross
Soldier's Medal
Navy & Marine Corps Medal
Airman's Medal
Coast Guard Medal
Bronze Star Medal
Purple Heart
Defense Meritorious Service Medal
Meritorious Service Medal
Air Medal
Aerial Achievement Medal
Joint Service Commendation Medal
Army Commendation Medal
Navy & Marine Corps Commendat'n Medal
Air Force Commendation Medal
Coast Guard Commendation Medal
Transportation 9-11 Medal
Joint Service Achievement Medal
Army Achievement Medal
Navy & Marine Corps Achievement Medal
Air Force Achievement Medal
Coast Guard Achievement Medal
Coast Guard Commandant's Letter of Commendation Ribbon
Combat Action Ribbon (Navy, Marine Corps)
Air Force Combat Action Medal
Combat Action Ribbon (Coast Guard)

Gold Lifesaving Medal
Silver Lifesaving Medal
Non Military Decorations
Prisoner of War Medal
Air Force Combat Readiness Medal
Army Good Conduct Medal
Reserve Special Commendation Ribbon
Navy Good Conduct Medal
Marine Corps Good Conduct Medal
Air Force Good Conduct Medal
Space Force Good Conduct Medal
Coast Guard Good Conduct Medal
Army Reserve Components Achievement Medal
Naval Reserve Meritorious Service Medal
Selected Marine Corps Reserve Medal
Air Reserve Forces Meritorious Service Medal
Coast Guard Reserve Good Conduct Medal
Coast Guard Enlisted Person of the Year Ribbon
Navy Fleet Marine Force Ribbon

Outstanding Airman of the Year Ribbon
Air Force Recognition Ribbon
Navy Expeditionary Medal
Marine Corps Expeditionary Medal
China Service Medal
American Defense Service Medal
Women's Army Corps Service Medal
American Campaign Medal
Asiatic-Pacific Campaign Medal
European-African-Middle Eastern Campaign Medal
World War II Victory Medal
Army of Occupation Medal
Navy Occupation Service Medal
Medal for Humane Action
National Defense Service Medal
Korean Service Medal
Antarctica Service Medal
Coast Guard Arctic Service Medal
Armed Forces Expeditionary Medal
Vietnam Service Medal
Southwest Asia Service Medal
Kosovo Campaign Medal
Afghanistan Campaign Medal
Iraq Campaign Medal
Inherent Resolve Campaign Medal
Global War on Terrorism Expeditionary Medal
Global War on Terrorism Service Medal
Korea Defense Service Medal
Armed Forces Service Medal
Humanitarian Service Medal
Military Outstanding Volunteer Service Medal
Military Army Sea Duty Ribbon
Armed Forces Reserve Medal
Army N.C.O. Professional Development Ribbon
Army Service Ribbon
Army Overseas Service Ribbon
Army Reserve Components Overseas Training Ribbon
Navy Sea Service Deployment Ribbon
Navy Arctic Service Ribbon
Naval Reserve Sea Service Deploy. Ribbon
Navy & Marine Corps Overseas Service Ribbon
Navy Recruiting Service Ribbon
Navy Accession Training Service Ribbon
Navy Ceremonial Duty Ribbon
Navy BMT Honor Graduate Ribbon
Naval Reserve Medal
Marine Corps Recruiting Ribbon
Marine Corps Drill Instructor Ribbon
Marine Corps Security Guard Ribbon
Marine Corps Combat Instructor Ribbon
Marine Corps Reserve Ribbon
Remote Combat Effects Medal
Air Force Air & Space Campaign Medal
Air Force Nuclear Deterrence Opn Medal
Air Force Overseas Ribbon (Short Tour)
Air Force Overseas Ribbon (Long Tour)
Air Force Expeditionary Service Ribbon
Air Force Special Duty Ribbon
Air Force Military Training Instructor

Air Force Recruiter Ribbon
Air Force N.C.O. Professional Military Education Graduate Ribbon
Air Force Basic Military Training Honor Graduate Ribbon
Air Force Training Ribbon
Transportation 9-11 Ribbon
Coast Guard Special Operations Service Ribbon
Coast Guard Sea Service Ribbon
Coast Guard Restricted Duty Ribbon
Coast Guard Overseas Service Ribbon
Coast Guard Basic Training Honor Graduate Ribbon
Coast Guard Recruiting Service Ribbon

Foreign Decorations and Medals
RVN Gallantry Cross (Foreign)
NATO Meritorious Service
Philippine Defense Medal
Philippine Liberation Medal
Philippine Independence Medal
United Nations Korean Service Medal
Inter-American Defense Board Medal
United Nations Medal
NATO Medal for Bosnia
NATO Medal for Kosovo
NATO Article 5 & Non-Article 5 Medals
Multinational Force & Observers Medal
Republic of Vietnam Campaign Medal
Kuwait Liberation Medal (Saudi Arabia)
Kuwait Liberation Medal (Kuwait)
Korean War Service Medal

UNIT CITATIONS (Right Breast):

Army Presidential Unit Citation
Air Force Presidential Unit Citation
Navy Presidential Unit Citation
Coast Guard Presidential Unit Citation Joint Joint Meritorious Unit Award
Army Valorous Unit Award
Navy Unit Commendation
Air Force Gallant Unit Citation
Coast Guard Unit Commendation
Army Meritorious Unit Commendation
Navy Meritorious Unit Commendation
Air Force Meritorious Unit Award
USCG Meritorious Unit Commendation
Army Superior Unit Award
Air Force Outstanding Unit Award
USCG Meritorious Team Commendation
Navy "E" Ribbon
Air Force Organizational Excellence Award
Coast Guard "E" Ribbon

Philippine Presidential Unit Citation
Korean Presidential Unit Citation
Vietnam Presidential Unit Citation
Vietnam Gallantry Cross Unit Citation
Vietnam Civil Actions Unit Citation

The following awards may not be worn on Army Uniform

Air Force Longevity Service Award
Navy Rifle Marksmanship Medal or Ribbon
Navy Pistol Marksmanship Medal or Ribbon
Coast Guard Rifle Marksmanship Medal or Ribbon
Coast Guard Pistol Marksmanship Medal or Ribbon
Air Force Small Arms Expert Marksmanship Ribbon

Copyright © Medals of America Press

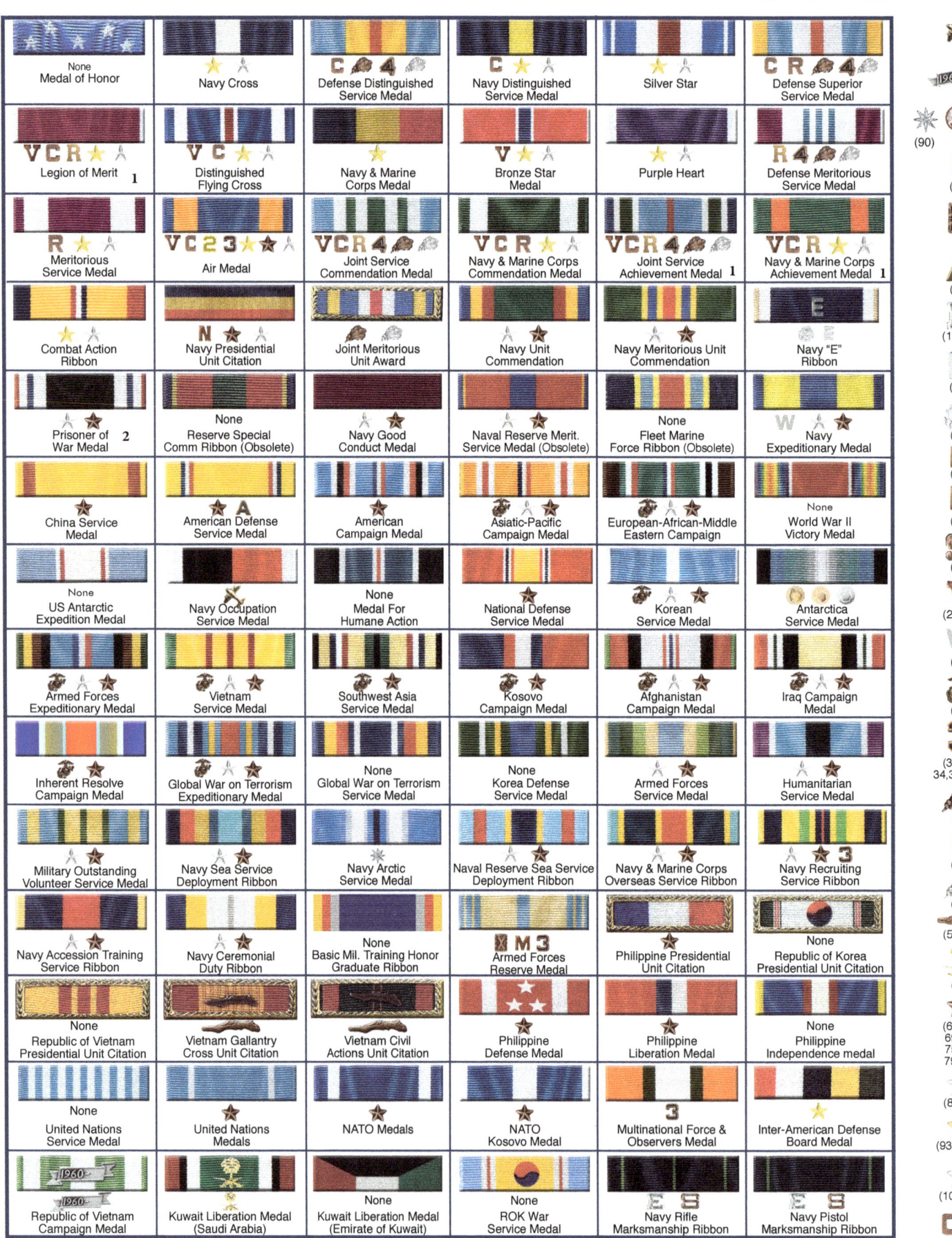

Navy Order of Precedence *(Other Services in Italics)*

Medal of Honor (Navy, Army, Air Force)
Navy Cross
Distinguished Service Cross
Air Force Cross
Coast Guard Cross
Defense Distinguished Service Medal
Navy Distinguished Service Medal
Army Distinguished Service Medal
Air Force Distinguished Service Medal
Homeland Security Dist. Service Medal
Transportation Distinguished Service Medal
Coast Guard Distinguished Service Medal
Silver Star
Defense Superior Service Medal
Legion of Merit
Distinguished Flying Cross
Navy & Marine Corps Medal
Soldier's Medal
Airman's Medal
Coast Guard Medal
Bronze Star Medal
Purple Heart
Defense Meritorious Service Medal
Meritorious Service Medal
Air Medal
Aerial Achievement Medal
Joint Service Commendation Medal
Navy & Marine Corps Commendat'n Medal
Army Commendation Medal
Air Force Commendation Medal
Coast Guard Commendation Medal
Transportation 9-11 Medal
Joint Service Achievement Medal
Navy & Marine Corps Achievement Medal
Army Achievement Medal
Air Force Achievement Medal
Coast Guard Achievement Medal
Combat Action Ribbon (Navy, Marine Corps)
Air Force Combat Action Medal
Combat Action Ribbon (Coast Guard)

Navy Presidential Unit Citation
Army Presidential Unit Citation
Air Force Presidential Unit Citation
Coast Guard Presidential Unit Citation
Joint Meritorious Unit Award
Army Valorous Unit Award
Air Force Gallant Unit Citation
Navy Unit Commendation
Navy Meritorious Unit Commendation
Army Meritorious Unit Commendation
Air Force Meritorious Unit Award
Air Force Outstanding Unit Award
Air Force Organizational Excellence Award
Army Superior Unit Award
D.O.T. Secretary's Outstanding Unit Award
Coast Guard Unit Commendation
Coast Guard Meritorious Unit Commendat'n
Coast Guard Meritorious Team Commendat'n
Navy "E" Ribbon
Coast Guard "E" Ribbon
Coast Guard Bicentennial Unit Commendat'n
Reserve Special Commendation Ribbon
Navy Good Conduct Medal

Marine Corps Good Conduct Medal
Army Good Conduct Medal
Gold Lifesaving Medal
Silver Lifesaving Medal
Non Military/DOD Decorations
Prisoner of War Medal
Air Force Good Conduct Medal
Space Force Good Conduct Medal
Coast Guard Good Conduct Medal
Naval Reserve Meritorious Service Medal
Selected Marine Corps Reserve Medal
Army Reserve Components Achievement Medal
Air Reserve Forces Meritorious Service Medal
Coast Guard Reserve Good Conduct Medal
Coast Guard Enlisted Person of the Year Ribbon
Navy Fleet Marine Force Ribbon

Navy Expeditionary Medal
Marine Corps Expeditionary Medal
China Service Medal
American Defense Service Medal
Women's Army Corps Service Medal
American Campaign Medal
European-African-Middle Eastern Campaign- Medal
Asiatic-Pacific Campaign Medal
World War II Victory Medal
U.S. Antarctic Expedition Medal
Navy Occupation Service Medal
Army of Occupation Medal
Medal for Humane Action
National Defense Service Medal
Korean Service Medal
Antarctica Service Medal
Coast Guard Arctic Service Medal
Armed Forces Expeditionary Medal
Vietnam Service Medal
Southwest Asia Service Medal
Kosovo Campaign Medal
Afghanistan Campaign Medal
Iraq Campaign Medal
Inherent Resolve Campaign Medal
Global War on Terrorism Expeditionary Medal
Global War on Terrorism Service Medal
Korea Defense Service Medal
Armed Forces Service Medal
Humanitarian Service Medal
Outstanding Volunteer Service Medal
Navy Sea Service Deployment Ribbon
Navy Arctic Service Ribbon
Naval Reserve Sea Service Deploy. Ribbon
Navy & Marine Corps Overseas Service Ribbon
Navy Recruiting Service Ribbon
Marine Corps Recruiting Ribbon
Marine Corps Drill Instructor Ribbon
Marine Security Guard Ribbon
Marine Combat Instructor Ribbon
Navy Accessions Training Service Ribbon
Navy Ceremonial Duty Ribbon
Navy BMT Honor Graduate Ribbon
Transportation 9-11 Ribbon

Coast Guard Restricted Duty Ribbon
Coast Guard Overseas Service Ribbon
Coast Guard Basic Training Honor Graduate Ribbon
Coast Guard Recruiting Service Ribbon
Air Force Remote Combat Effects Medal
Air Force Air & Space Campaign Medal
Air Force Nuclear Deterrence Operations Medal
Air Force Overseas Ribbon (Short Tour)
Air Force Overseas Ribbon (Long Tour)
Air Force Expeditionary Service Ribbon
Air Force Longevity Service Award Ribbon
Air Force Air & Space Special Duty Ribbon
Air Force Military Training Instructor Ribbon
Air Force Recruiter Ribbon
Army Sea Duty Ribbon
Armed Forces Reserve Medal
Naval Reserve Medal
Marine Corps Reserve Ribbon
Army N.C.O. Professional Development Ribbon
Army Service Ribbon
Army Overseas Service Ribbon
Army Reserve Components Overseas Training Ribbon
Air Force N.C.O. Professional Military Education Graduate Ribbon
Air Force Basic Military Training Honor Graduate Ribbon
Air Force Recruiter Ribbon
Air Force Small Arms Expert Marksmanship Ribbon
Air Force Training Ribbon

Foreign Decorations and Medals
RVN Gallantry Cross (Foreign)
NATO Meritorious Service
Philippine Defense Medal
Philippine Liberation Medal
Philippine Independence Medal
United Nations Korean Service Medal
Inter-American Defense Board Medal
United Nations Medal
NATO Medal for Bosnia
NATO Medal for Kosovo
NATO Article 5 & Non-Article 5 Medals
Multinational Force & Observers Medal
Republic of Vietnam Campaign Medal
Kuwait Liberation Medal (Saudi Arabia)
Kuwait Liberation Medal (Kuwait)
Korean War Service Medal

Navy Rifle Marksmanship Medal
Navy Pistol Marksmanship Medal
Coast Guard Rifle Marksmanship Medal
Coast Guard Pistol Marksmanship Medal

The following awards may not be worn on the Navy Uniform

Coast Guard Commandant's Letter of Commendation Ribbon
Air Force Combat Readiness Medal

Outstanding Airman of the Year Ribbon
Air Force Recognition Ribbon

Copyright © Medals of America Press

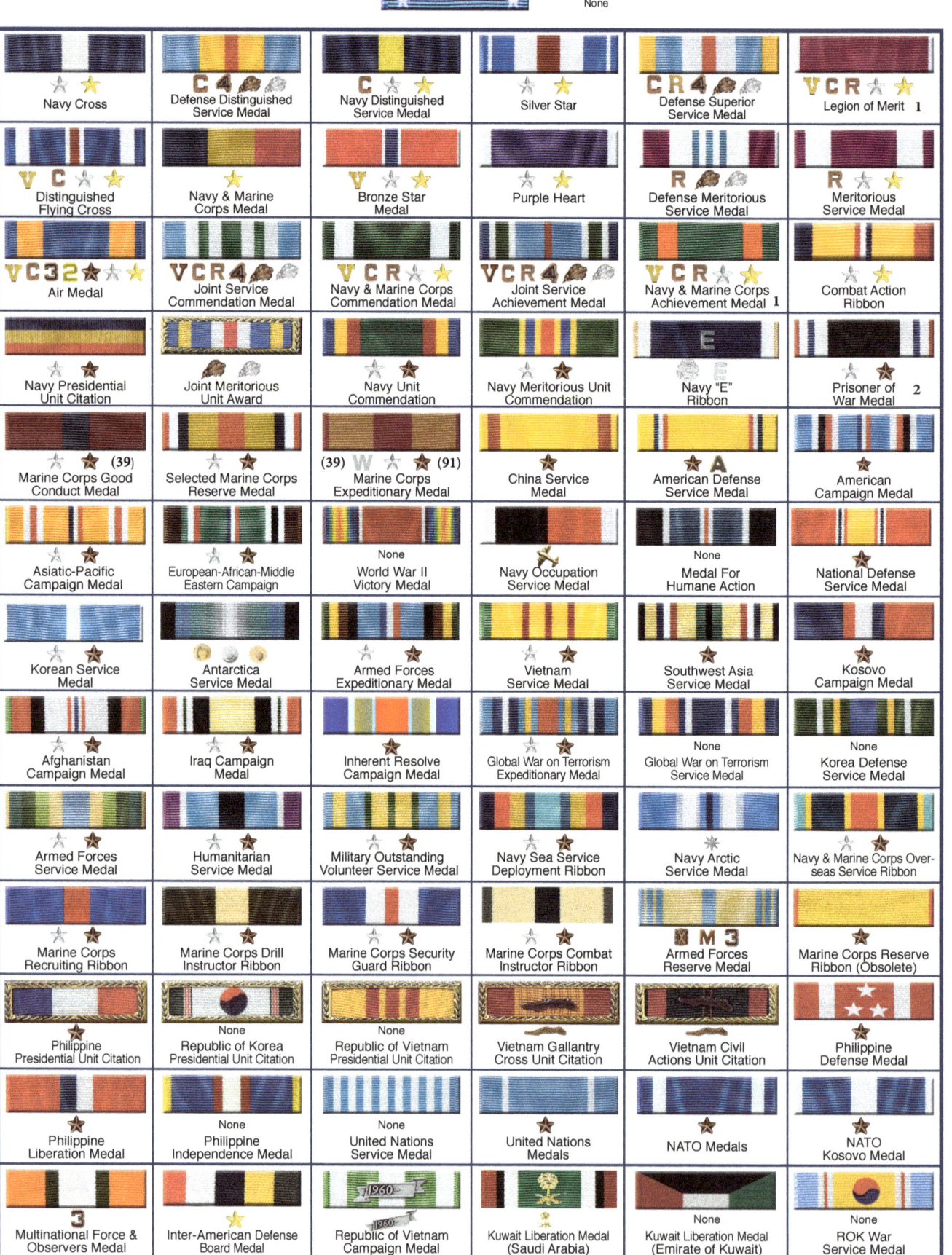

Marine Corps Order of Precedence *(Other Services in Italics)*

Medal of Honor (Navy, Army, Air Force)
Navy Cross
Distinguished Service Cross
Air Force Cross
Coast Guard Cross
Defense Distinguished Service Medal
Navy Distinguished Service Medal
Army Distinguished Service Medal
Air Force Distinguished Service Medal
Homeland Security Dist. Service Medal
Transportation Distinguished Service Medal
Coast Guard Distinguished Service Medal
Silver Star
Defense Superior Service Medal
Legion of Merit
Distinguished Flying Cross
Navy & Marine Corps Medal
Soldier's Medal
Airman's Medal
Coast Guard Medal
Bronze Star Medal
Purple Heart
Defense Meritorious Service Medal
Meritorious Service Medal
Air Medal
Aerial Achievement Medal
Joint Service Commendation Medal
Navy & Marine Corps Commendat'n Medal
Army Commendation Medal
Air Force Commendation Medal
Coast Guard Commendation Medal
Transportation 9-11 Medal
Joint Service Achievement Medal
Navy & Marine Corps Achievement Medal
Army Achievement Medal
Air Force Achievement Medal
Coast Guard Achievement Medal
Combat Action Ribbon (Navy, Marine Corps)
Air Force Combat Action Medal
Combat Action Ribbon (Coast Guard)

Navy Presidential Unit Citation
Army Presidential Unit Citation
Air Force Presidential Unit Citation
Coast Guard Presidential Unit Citation
Joint Meritorious Unit Award
Army Valorous Unit Award
Air Force Gallant Unit Citation
Navy Unit Commendation
Navy Meritorious Unit Commendation
Army Meritorious Unit Commendation
Air Force Meritorious Unit Award
Air Force Outstanding Unit Award
Air Force Organizational Excellence Award
Army Superior Unit Award
D.O.T. Secretary's Outstanding Unit Award
Coast Guard Unit Commendation
Coast Guard Meritorious Unit Commendat'n

Coast Guard Meritorious Team Commendation
Navy "E" Ribbon
Coast Guard "E" Ribbon
Gold Lifesaving Medal
Silver Lifesaving Medal
NON-DOD U.S. Decorations
Prisoner of War Medal
Air Force Combat Readiness Medal
Reserve Special Commendation Ribbon
Marine Corps Good Conduct Medal
Navy Good Conduct Medal
Army Good Conduct Medal
Air Force Good Conduct Medal
Space Force Good Conduct Medal
Coast Guard Good Conduct Medal
Selected Marine Corps Reserve Medal
Army Reserve Components Achievement Medal
Naval Reserve Meritorious Service Medal
Air Reserve Forces Meritorious Service Medal
Coast Guard Reserve Good Conduct Medal
Coast Guard Enlisted Person of the Year Ribbon
Navy Fleet Marine Force Ribbon
Marine Corps Expeditionary Medal
Navy Expeditionary Medal
China Service Medal
American Defense Service Medal
Women's Army Corps Service Medal
American Campaign Medal
European-African-Middle Eastern Campaign Medal
Asiatic-Pacific Campaign Medal
World War II Victory Medal
U.S. Antarctic Expedition Medal
Navy Occupation Service Medal
Army of Occupation Medal
Medal for Humane Action
National Defense Service Medal
Korean Service Medal
Antarctica Service Medal
Coast Guard Arctic Service Medal
Armed Forces Expeditionary Medal
Vietnam Service Medal
Southwest Asia Service Medal
Kosovo Campaign Medal
Afghanistan Campaign Medal
Iraq Campaign Medal
Inherent Resolve Campaign Medal
Global War on Terrorism Expeditionary Medal
Global War on Terrorism Service Medal
Korea Defense Service Medal
Armed Forces Service Medal
Humanitarian Service Medal
Military Outstanding Volunteer Service Medal
Navy Sea Service Deployment Ribbon

Navy Arctic Service Ribbon
Naval Reserve Sea Service Deployment Ribbon
Navy & Marine Corps Overseas Service Ribbon
Marine Corps Recruiting Ribbon
Marine Corps Drill Instructor Ribbon
Marine Corps Security Guard Ribbon
Marine Corps Combat Instructor Ribbon
Navy Recruiting Service Ribbon
Navy Accession Training Service Ribbon
Navy Ceremonial Duty Ribbon
Navy BMT Honor Graduate Ribbon
Air Force Air & Space Campaign Medal
Air Force Nuclear Deterrence Operation Medal
Air Force Overseas Ribbon (Short Tour)
Air Force Overseas Ribbon (Long Tour)
Air Force Expeditionary Service Ribbon Air Force special Duty Ribbon
Air Force Military Training Instructor Ribbon
Air Force Recruiter Ribbon
Transportation 9-11 Ribbon
Coast Guard Special Operations Service Ribbon
Coast Guard Sea Service Ribbon
Coast Guard Restricted Duty Ribbon
Coast Guard Basic Training Honor Graduate Ribbon
Coast Guard Recruiting Service Ribbon
Army Sea Duty Ribbon
Armed Forces Reserve Medal
Army Overseas Service Ribbon
Naval Reserve Medal
Marine Corps Reserve Ribbon

Foreign Decorations and Medals
RVN Gallantry Cross (Foreign)
NATO Meritorious Service
Philippine Defense Medal
Philippine Liberation Medal
Philippine Independence Medal
United Nations Korean Service Medal
Inter-American Defense Board Medal
United Nations Medal
NATO Medal for Bosnia
NATO Medal for Kosovo
NATO Article 5 & Non-Article 5 Medals
Multinational Force & Observers Medal
Republic of Vietnam Campaign Medal
Kuwait Liberation Medal (Saudi Arabia)
Kuwait Liberation Medal (Kuwait)
Korean War Service Medal

The following awards may not be worn on the Marine Corps Uniform

Coast Guard Commandant's Letter of Commendation Ribbon
Coast Guard Bicentennial Unit Commen
Army N.C.O. Professional Development Ribbon
Army Service Ribbon
Army Reserve Components Overseas Training Ribbon

Air Force Longevity Service Award
Air Force N.C.O. Professional Military Education Graduate Ribbon
Air Force Basic Military Training Honor Graduate Ribbon
Air Force Small Arms Expert Marksmanship Ribbon
Air Force Training Ribbon

Navy Rifle Marksmanship Medal/Ribbon
Navy Pistol Marksmanship Medal/Ribbon
Coast Guard Rifle Marksmanship Medal/Ribbon
Coast Guard Pistol Marksmanship Medal/Ribbon

Copyright © Medals of America Press

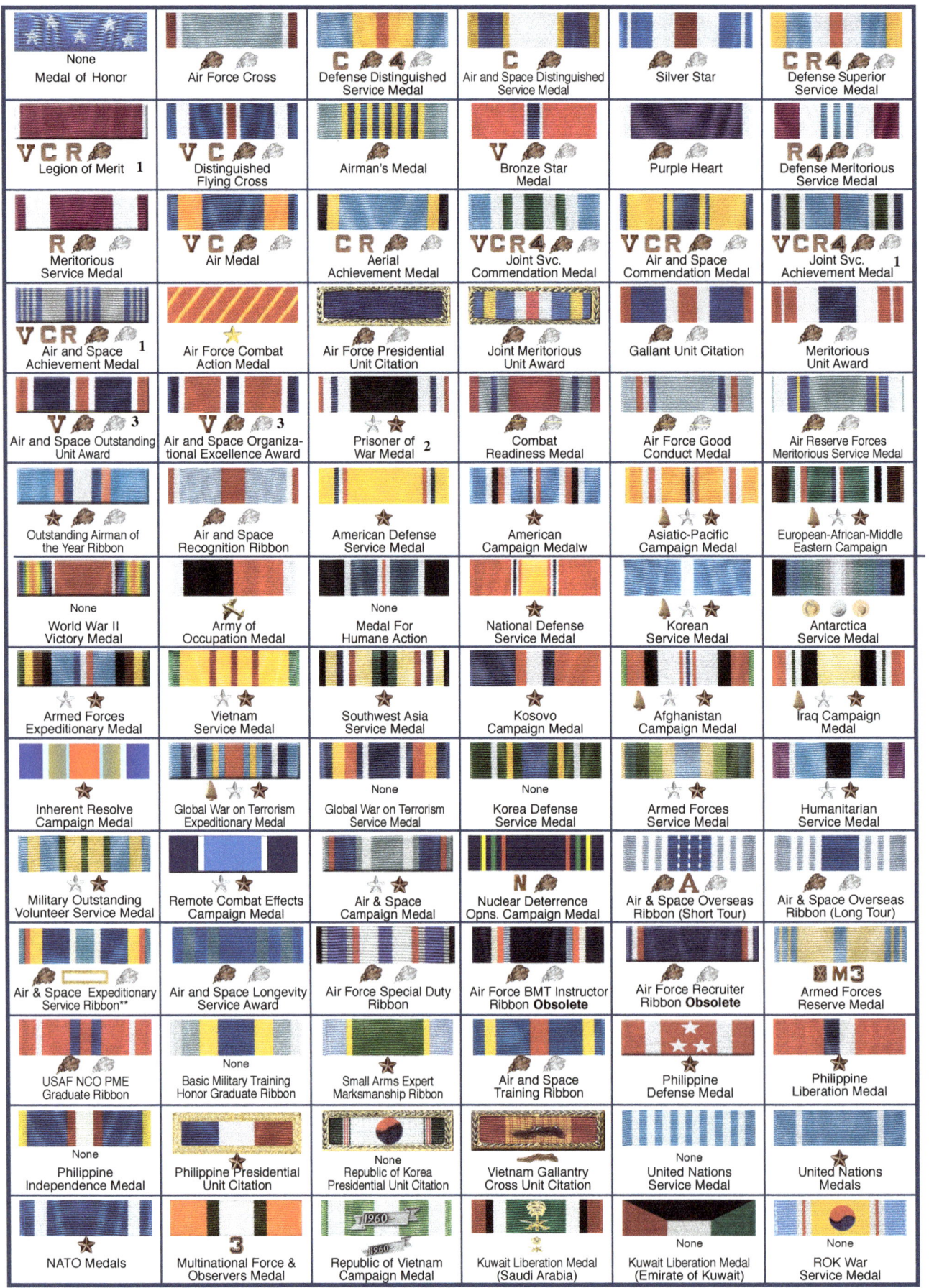

Air Force Order of Precedence *(Other Services in Italics)*

Medal of Honor (Air Force, Army, Navy)
Air Force Cross
Distinguished Service Cross
Navy Cross
Coast Guard Cross
Defense Distinguished Service Medal
Air Force Distinguished Service Medal
Army Distinguished Service Medal
Navy Distinguished Service Medal
Homeland Security Dist. Service Medal
    Transportation Distinguished Service Medal
Coast Guard Distinguished Service Medal
Silver Star
Defense Superior Service Medal
Legion of Merit
Distinguished Flying Cross
Airman's Medal
Soldier's Medal
Navy & Marine Corps Medal
Coast Guard Medal
Bronze Star Medal
Purple Heart
    Defense Meritorious Service Medal
Meritorious Service Medal
Air Medal
Aerial Achievement Medal
Joint Service Commendation Medal
Air Force Commendation Medal
Army Commendation Medal
Navy & Marine Corps Commendat'n Medal
Coast Guard Commendation Medal
Transportation 9-11 Medal
Joint Service Achievement Medal
Air Force Achievement Medal
Army Achievement Medal
Navy & Marine Corps Achievement Medal
Coast Guard Achievement Medal
Coast Guard Commandant's Letter of
    Commendation Ribbon
Combat Action Ribbon (Navy, Marine Corps)
Air Force Combat Action Medal
Combat Action Ribbon (Coast Guard)
Air Force Presidential Unit Citation
Army Presidential Unit Citation
Navy Presidential Unit Citation
Coast Guard Presidential Unit Citation
Joint Meritorious Unit Award
Army Valorous Unit Award
Air Force Gallant Unit Citation
D.O.T. Secretary's Outstanding Unit Award
Coast Guard Unit Commendation
Navy Unit Commendation
Coast Guard Meritorious Unit Commendation
Coast Guard Meritorious Team Commendation
Army Meritorious Unit Commendation
Navy Meritorious Unit Commendation
Air Force Meritorious Unit Award
Air Force Outstanding Unit Award
Air Force Organizatonal Excellence Award
Army Superior Unit Award
Navy "E" Ribbon
Coast Guard "E" Ribbon
Coast Guard Bicentennial Unit Commendation
Gold Lifesaving Medal
    Silver Lifesaving Medal
Non- DoD Decorations
Prisoner of War Medal
Air Force Combat Readiness Medal

Air Force Good Conduct Medal
Space Force Good Conduct Medal
Army Good Conduct Medal
Reserve Special Commendation Ribbon
Navy Good Conduct Medal
Marine Corps Good Conduct Medal
    Coast Guard Good Conduct Medal
Air Reserve Forces Meritorious Service
    Medal
Army Reserve Components Achievement
    Medal
Naval Reserve Meritorious Service Medal
Selected Marine Corps Reserve Medal
Coast Guard Reserve Good Conduct Medal
Coast Guard Enlisted Person of the Year
    Ribbon
Navy Fleet Marine Force Ribbon
Outstanding Airman of the Year Ribbon
    Air Force Recognition Ribbon

Navy Expeditionary Medal
Marine Corps Expeditionary Medal
China Service Medal
American Defense Service Medal
Women's Army Corps Service Medal
American Campaign Medal
Asiatic-Pacific Campaign Medal
European-African-Middle Eastern
    Campaign Medal
World War II Victory Medal
Army of Occupation Medal
Navy Occupation Service Medal
    Medal for Humane Action
    National Defense Service Medal
    Korean Service Medal
    Antarctica Service Medal
Coast Guard Arctic Service Medal
    Armed Forces Expeditionary Medal
    Vietnam Service Medal
    Southwest Asia Service Medal
    Kosovo Campaign Medal
Afghanistan Campaign Medal
Iraq Campaign Medal
Inherent Resolve Campaign Medal
Global War on Terrorism Expeditionary Medal
    Global War on Terrorism Service Medal
    Korea Defense Service Medal
    Armed Forces Service Medal
    Humanitarian Service Medal
Military Outstanding Volunteer Service Medal
Air & Space Remote Effects Campaign Medal
Air & Space Campaign Medal
Air & Space Nuclear Deterrence Operations
    Medal
    Air & Space Overseas Ribbon (Short Tour)
    Air & Space Overseas Ribbon (Long Tour)
    Air & Space Expeditionary Service Ribbon
Army Overseas Service Ribbon
    Army Reserve Components Overseas
    Training Ribbon
Sea Service Deployment Ribbon
    Navy Arctic Service Ribbon
    Naval Reserve Sea Service Deploy. Ribbon
    Navy & Marine Corps Overseas
    Service Ribbon
    Navy Recruiting Service Ribbon
    Navy Accession Training Service Ribbon

Navy Ceremonial Duty Ribbon
Navy BMT Honor Graduate Ribbon
Marine Corps Recruiting Ribbon
Marine Corps Drill Instructor Ribbon
Marine Corps Security Guard Ribbon
Marine Corps Combat Instructor Ribbon
Transportation 9-11 Ribbon
Coast Guard Special Operations
    Service Medal
Coast Guard Sea Service Ribbon
Coast Guard Restricted Duty Ribbon
Coast Guard Overseas Service Ribbon
Air Force Longevity Service Award
    Air Force Special Duty Ribbon
Air Force Military Training Instructor
    Ribbon
Air Force Recruiter Ribbon
Army Sea Duty Ribbon
Armed Forces Reserve Medal
Naval Reserve Medal
Marine Corps Reserve Ribbon
Air Force N.C.O. Professional Military
    Education Graduate Ribbon
Army N.C.O. Professional Development
    Ribbon
    Air Force Basic Military Training
    Honor Graduate Ribbon
Coast Guard Basic Training Honor
    Graduate Ribbon
Coast Guard Recruiting Service
    Ribbon
Air Force Small Arms Expert Marksmanship
    Ribbon
Air and Space Training Ribbon

Foreign Decorations and Medals
RVN Gallantry Cross (Foreign)
NATO Meritorious Service
Philippine Defense Medal
Philippine Liberation Medal
Philippine Independence Medal
United Nations Korean Service Medal
Inter-American Defense Board Medal
United Nations Medal
NATO Medal for Bosnia
NATO Medal for Kosovo
NATO Article 5 & Non-Article 5 Medals
Multinational Force & Observers Medal
Republic of Vietnam Campaign Medal
Kuwait Liberation Medal (Saudi Arabia)
Kuwait Liberation Medal (Kuwait)
Korean War Service Medal

Navy Rifle Marksmanship Medal/Ribbon
Navy Pistol Marksmanship Medal/Ribbon
Coast Guard Rifle Marksmanship
    Medal/Ribbon
Coast Guard Pistol Marksmanship
    Medal/Ribbon

No Specific Restrictions in Air Force Uniform or Award Regulations.

Copyright © Medals of America Press

Current U.S. Space Force Ribbons & Devices

Correct Order of Ribbon Wear

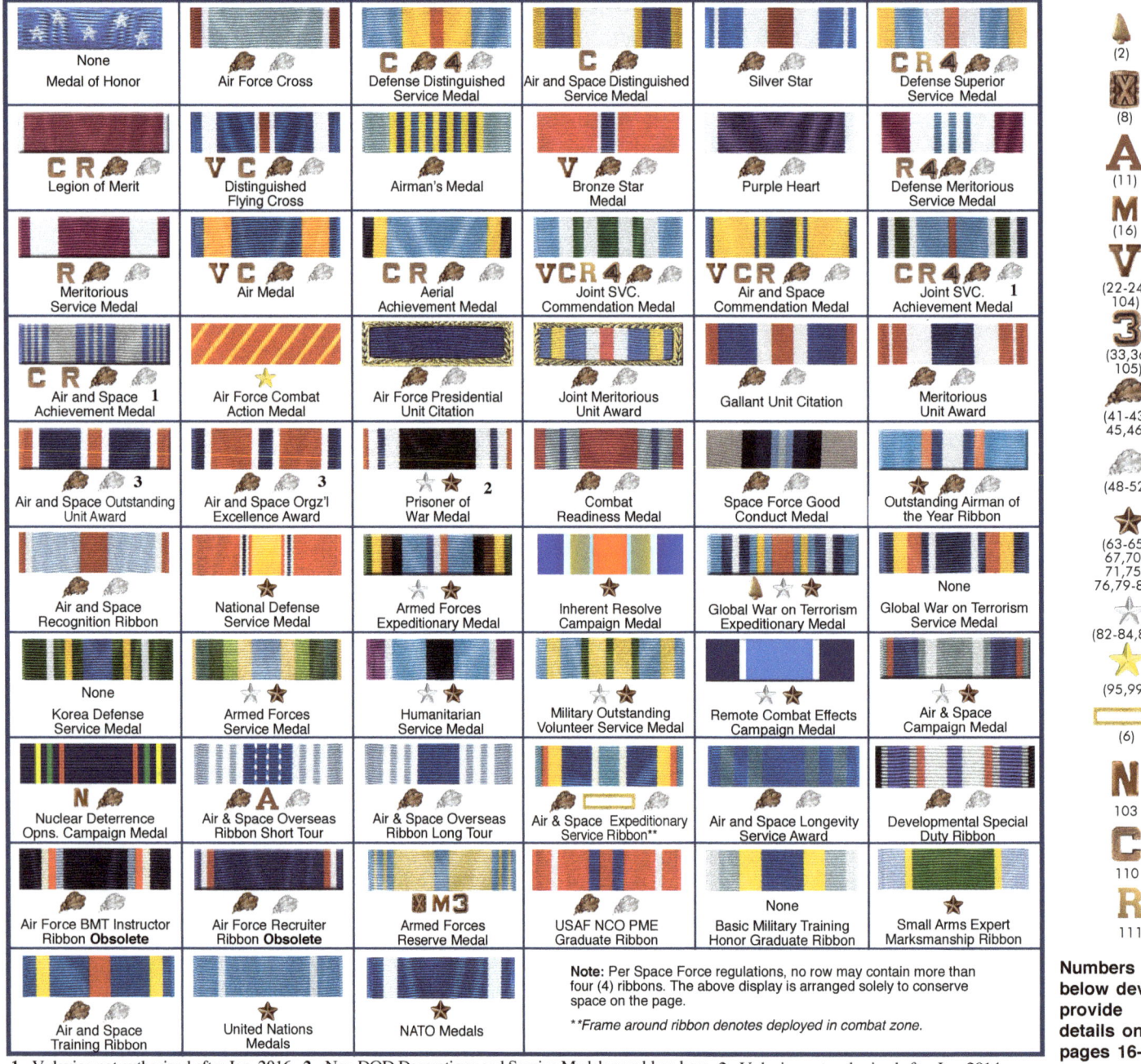

1 - V device not authorized after Jan. 2016. 2 - Non DOD Decorations and Service Medals would go here. 3 - V device not authorized after Jan. 2014.

Space Force Order of Precedence

Think of the Space Force as having the same relationship to Air Force as the Marine Corps has to the Navy. Basically the Space Force originated from the Air Force Space Command in 2019, so like the Marine Corps it needed its own Good Conduct Medal but shares the Air Force and Dept. of Defense Awards system.

Coast Guard Order of Precedence

The Coast Guard which comes under the command of the Navy during war time follows the Navy order of precedence except as shown to the right.

The following awards may not be worn on the Coast Guard Uniform

Air and Space Force Training Ribbon
Army Service Ribbon
Army N.C.O. Professional Development Ribbon
Air Force N.C.O. Professional Military Education Graduate Ribbon

Outstanding Airman of the Year Ribbon
Air and Space Recognition Ribbon
Air Force Combat Readiness Medal
Air and Space Longevity Service Award Ribbon

Air Force Small Arms Expert Marksmanship Ribbon
Navy Rifle Marksmanship Ribbon
Navy Pistol Marksmanship Ribbon

12 Military Ribbon Guide

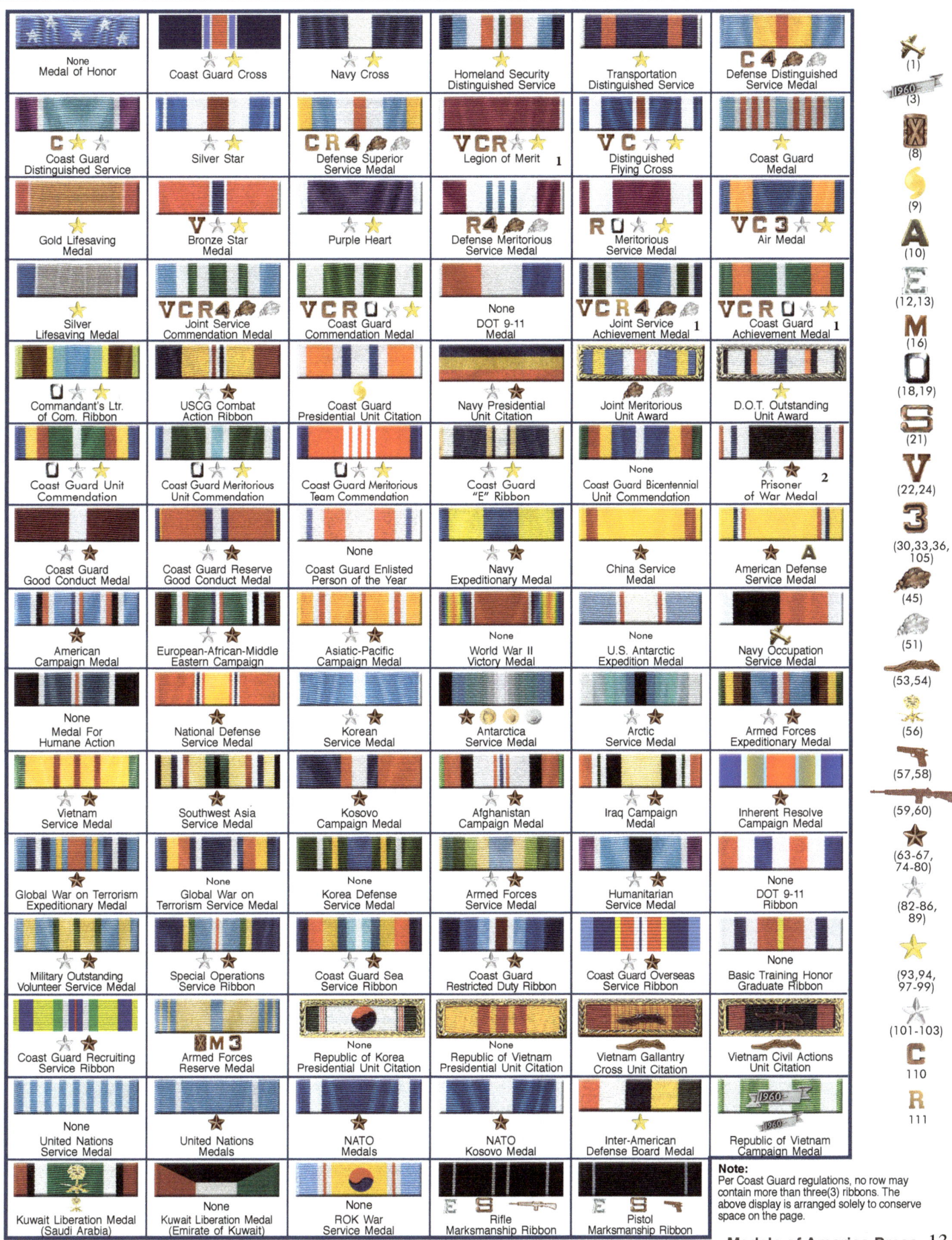

Right Breast Displays on Full Dress Uniforms

The three Naval Services prescribe the wear of "ribbon only" awards on the right breast of the full dress uniform when large medals are worn. The Navy and Coast Guard align their ribbons inboard to outboard while the Marines align theirs outboard to inboard. The Philippine Defense Ribbon, Philippine Liberation Ribbon and the Philippine Independence Ribbon are now classified as Medals.

U.S. Navy

Navy Presidential Unit Citation		Combat Action Ribbon	
Navy Meritorious Unit Commendation	Navy Unit Commendation	Joint Meritorious Unit Award
Fleet Marine Force Ribbon	Reserve Special Commendation Ribbon	Navy "E" Ribbon
Navy Reserve Sea Service Service Deployment Ribbon	Arctic Service Ribbon	Sea Service Deployment Ribbon
Navy Accession Training Service Ribbon	Navy Recruiting Service Ribbon	Navy & Marine Corps Overseas Service Ribbon
Philippine Presidential Unit Citation	Navy BMT Honor Graduate Ribbon	Navy Ceremonial Duty Ribbon
Vietnam Gallantry Cross Unit Citation	Vietnam Presidential Unit Citation	Korean Presidential Unit Ribbon
Pistol Marksmanship Ribbon	Rifle Marksmanship Ribbon	Vietnam Civil Actions Unit Citation

U.S. Marine Corps

	Combat Action Ribbon	
Navy Presidential Unit Citation	Joint Meritorious Unit Award	Navy Unit Commendation
Navy Meritorious Unit Commendation	Navy "E" Ribbon	Sea Service Deployment Ribbon
Arctic Service Ribbon	Navy & Marine Corps Overseas Service Ribbon	Marine Corps Recruiting Ribbon
Marine Corps Drill Instructor Ribbon	Marine Corps Security Guard Ribbon	Marine Corps Combat Instructor Ribbon
Marine Corps Reserve Ribbon	Philippine Presidential Unit Citation	Korean Presidential Unit Citation
Vietnam Presidential Unit Citation	Vietnam Gallantry Cross Unit Citation	Vietnam Civil Actions Unit Citation

U.S. Coast Guard

Coast Guard Combat Action Ribbon		Commandant's Letter of Commendation Ribbon	
Joint Meritorious Unit Award	Navy Presidential Unit Citation	Coast Guard Presidential Unit Citation
Coast Guard Meritorious Unit Commendation	Coast Guard Unit Commendation	D.O.T. Outstanding Unit Award
Coast Guard Bicentennial Unit Commendation	Coast Guard "E" Ribbon	Coast Guard Meritorious Team Commendation
Special Operations Service Ribbon	Transportation 9-11 Ribbon	Enlisted Person of the Year Ribbon
Coast Guard Overseas Service Ribbon	Restricted Duty Ribbon	Coast Guard Sea Service Ribbon
Philippine Presidential Unit Citation	Coast Guard Recruiting Service Ribbon	Basic Training Honor Graduate Ribbon
Vietnam Gallantry Cross Unit Citation	Vietnam Presidential Unit Citation	Korean Presidential Unit Citation
Coast Guard Pistol Marksmanship Ribbon	Coast Guard Rifle Marksmanship Ribbon	Vietnam Civil Actions Unit Citation

United Nations Ribbons for Wear on the U.S. Military Uniform

Originally, U.S. military personnel serving with United Nations Missions were permitted to wear only two UN medals, the United Nations Korean Service Medal and the United Nations Medal. However, changes in DOD policy brought the total to 28. Only one ribbon may be worn on the US military uniform and awards for any subsequent missions are denoted by the three-sixteenth inch bronze stars.

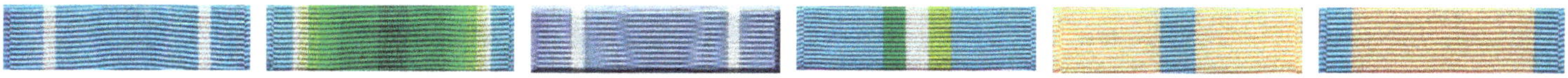

UNTSO Middle East	UNMOGIP India, Pakistan	UNOGIL Lebanon	UNSF/UNTEA West New Guinea	UNIKOM Iraq, Kuwait	MINURSO Western Sahara
UNAMIC Cambodia	UNPROFOR Former Yugoslavia	UNTAC Cambodia	UNOSOM II Somalia	UNMIH Haiti	UNSSM Special Service Medal

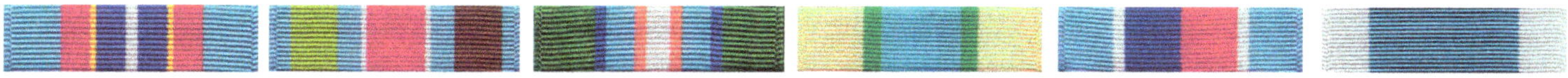

AUTHORIZED 30 SEPTEMBER 2011

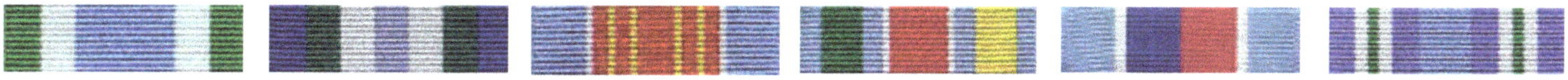

ONUMOZ Mozambique	UNOMIG Georgia	UNPREDEP Macedonia	UNTAES E. Slavonia, Baranja	UNSMIH Haiti	MINUGUA Guatemala
UNMIK Kosovo	UNTAET East Timor	MONUC Congo	UNMEE Ethiopia, Enitrea	UNMISET East Timor	UNMIL Liberia
MINUSTAH Haiti	UNAMID Darfur	MINURCAT Cent. Afr. Rep, Chad	MONUSCO Congo	UNAMI UN Assistance Mission in Iraq	

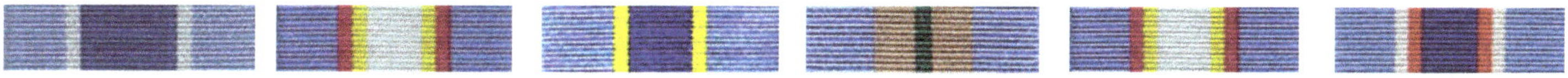

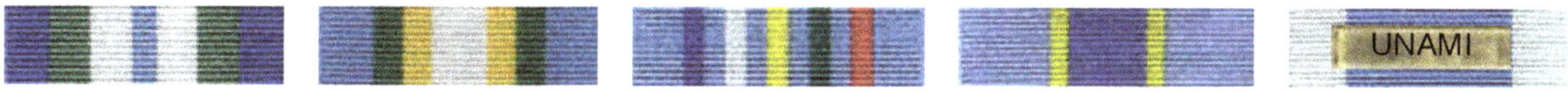

NATO Ribbons and Attachments

For the U.S. military, a bronze service star indicates additional awards of the service and mission-related NATO Medals. As of May 2013, only the NATO MSM ribbon bar (as a personal foreign decoration) and the basic NATO ribbon (as a non-US service and campaign medal) may be worn for U.S. services. The basic NATO Medal ribbon bar worn will be the first NATO campaign medal awarded, with subsequent campaigns indicated with a bronze service star.

Only the basic NATO Medal is authorized to be worn on the U.S. uniform. Personnel authorized subsequent awards will add a bronze service star to the basic NATO Medal or ribbon. For example, if you have been awarded the NATO Medal - Kosovo you would wear the NATO ribbon for Kosovo plus a bronze service star to denote award of the NATO Medal - ISAF. The NATO Medal is worn below the United Nations Medal.

NATO Meritorious Service Medal	NATO Article 5 Medal	NATO Non-Article 5 Medal	NATO Medal for the former Yugoslavia	NATO Medal for Kosovo
NATO Medal for Macadonia	NATO Article 5 Medal for Operation Eagle Assist	NATO Article 5 Medal for Operation Active Endeavor	Former design for NATO Non-Article 5 Medal for the Balkan	Bronze Service Star Denotes second and subsequent awards of a NATO service award or participation in a campaign or operation.

There are currently fourteen versions of the NATO Medal in existence and there are corresponding clasps for operations such as ISAF, Kosovo, the former Yugoslavia, NTM-I, and clasps designating Article 5, and Non-Article 5 designations etc. However, clasp are not authorized U.S. military personnel.

Armed Forces Ribbon Devices

1. Airplane, C-54, Gold

Services: All
Worn on: World War II Occupation Medals
Denotes: Service during Berlin Airlift *(1948-49)*

2. Arrowhead, Bronze

Services: Army, Air Force
Worn on: Campaign & Expeditionary awards since World War II
Denotes: Combat assault or invasion

3. Bar, Date, Silver

Services: All
Worn on: Republic of Vietnam Campaign Medal
Denotes: Worn upon initial issue; has no significance

4a. Bar, Knotted, Bronze

Services: Army
Worn on: Army Good Conduct Medal
Denotes: Additional periods of service *(awards 2 through 5)*

4b. Bar, Knotted, Silver

Services: Army
Worn on: Army Good Conduct Medal
Denotes: Additional periods of service *(awards 6 through 10)*

4c. Bar, Knotted, Gold

Services: Army
Worn on: Army Good Conduct Medal
Denotes: Additional periods of service *(awards 11 through 15)*

5a. Disk, Bronze

Services: All
Worn on: Antarctica Service Medal
Denotes: Wintered over on the Antarctic continent

5b. Disk, Gold

Services: All
Worn on: Antarctica Service Medal
Denotes: Wintered over twice on the Antarctic continent

5c. Disk, Silver

Services: All
Worn on: Antarctica Service Medal
Denotes: Wintered over three times on the Antarctic continent

6. Frame, Gold

Services: Air Force
Worn on: Expeditionary Service Ribbon
Denotes: Satisfactory participation in combat operations

7. Globe, Gold

Services: Navy
Worn on: Navy Presidential Unit Citation
Denotes: Service with USS Triton during 1st submerged cruise around the world

8a. Hourglass, Bronze

Services: All
Worn on: Armed Forces Reserve Medal
Denotes: 10 Years of service in the Reserve Forces

8b. Hourglass, Silver

Services: All
Worn on: Armed Forces Reserve Medal
Denotes: 20 Years of service in the Reserve Forces

8c. Hourglass, Gold

Services: All
Worn on: Armed Forces Reserve Medal
Denotes: 30 Years of service in the Reserve Forces

9. Hurricane Device, Gold

Services: Coast Guard
Worn on: USCG Presidential Unit Citation
Denotes: Service during the aftermath of Hurricane Katrina

10. Letter "A", Block, Bronze

Services: Navy, Marine Corps, Coast Guard
Worn on: American Defense Service Medal
Denotes: Atlantic Fleet service prior to World War II

11. Letter "A", Serif, Bronze

Services: Air Force
Worn on: Overseas Service Ribbon (Short Tour)
Denotes: Service at Thule Air Base above the Arctic Circle

12. Letter "E", Serif, Bronze

Services: Navy, Coast Guard
Worn on: Marksmanship Ribbons
Denotes: First "Expert" qualification *(Obsolete)*

13. Letter "E", Serif, Silver

Services: Navy, Coast Guard
Worn on: Marksmanship Ribbons
Denotes: "Expert" weapons qualification

14. Letter "E", Block, Silver

Services: Navy, Marine Corps
Worn on: Navy "E" Ribbon
Denotes: Initial and subsequent awards *(3 maximum)*

15. Letter "E", Wreathed, Silver

Services: Navy, Marine Corps
Worn on: Navy "E" Ribbon
Denotes: Fourth *(Final)* award

16. Letter "M", Block, Bronze

Services: All
Worn on: Armed Forces Reserve Medal
Denotes: Mobilization for active military service

17. Letter "N", Block, Gold

Services: Navy
Worn on: Navy Presidential Unit Citation
Denotes: Service aboard USS Nautilus during 1st cruise under the Arctic ice cap

18. Letter "O", Block, Silver

Services: Coast Guard
Worn on: Meritorious Service Medal and USCG decorations
Denotes: Distinguished operational service by individual

19. Letter "O", Block, Silver

Services: Coast Guard
Worn on: Coast Guard Unit Awards
Denotes: Distinguished operational service by cited unit

20. Letter "S", Serif, Bronze

Services: Navy
Worn on: Navy Marksmanship ribbons
Denotes: Sharpshooter qualification

21. Letter "S", Serif, Silver

Services: Coast Guard
Worn on: Coast Guard Marksmanship ribbons
Denotes: Sharpshooter qualification

22. Letter "V", Serif, Bronze

Services: All (Except Marine Corps)
Worn on: Personal decorations
Denotes: Valorous actions in combat

23. Letter "V", Serif, Bronze

Services: Air Force
Worn on: Outstanding Unit Award and Organizational Excellence Award **Obsolete**
Denotes: Valorous actions

24. Letter "V", Serif, Bronze

Services: All
Worn on: Joint Service Commendation Medal
Denotes: Valorous actions in combat

Armed Forces Ribbon Devices

25. Letter "V", Serif, Gold

Services: Marine Corps
Worn on: Personal Decorations
Denotes: Valorous actions in combat

26. Letter "W", Block, Silver

Services: Navy, Marine Corps.
Worn on: Expeditionary Medal Ribbon Bar
Denotes: Participation in the defense of Wake Island (Dec, 1941)

27. Maltese Cross, Bronze

Services: Navy
Worn on: World War I Victory Medal
Denotes: Service by Navy personnel with the AEF

28. FMF Device, Bronze

Services: Navy
Worn on: Campaign/ Exp. medals since World War II
Denotes: Service by Naval combat personnel with Marine Corps units

29a. Medal, Miniature, Gold

Services: Foreign military personnel
Worn on: Legion of Merit
Denotes: Level of award ("Chief Commander")

29b. Medal, Miniature, Silver

Services: Foreign military personnel
Worn on: Legion of Merit
Denotes: Level of award ("Commander")

29c. Medal, Miniature, Gold

Services: Foreign military personnel
Worn on: Legion of Merit
Denotes: Level of award ("Officer")

30. Numeral, Block, Bronze

Services: Navy, Marine Corps
Worn on: Air Medal
Denotes: Total number of Strike/Flight awards

31. Numeral, Block, Bronze

Services: Army
Worn on: Air Medal
Denotes: Total number of awards

32. Numeral, Block, Bronze

Services: All (Except Coast Guard)
Worn on: Humanitarian Service Medal
Denotes: Number of additional awards (Obsolete)

33. Numeral, Block, Bronze

Services: All
Worn on: Armed Forces Reserve Medal
Denotes: Number of times mobilized for active duty, M should be in middle.

34. Numeral, Block, Bronze

Services: Navy
Worn on: Navy Recruiting Service Ribbon
Denotes: Total number of "Gold Wreath" awards

35. Numeral, Block, Bronze

Services: Army
Worn on: Overseas Service and Reserve Components Overseas Training Ribbons
Denotes: Total number of awards

36. Numeral, Block, Bronze

Services: All
Worn on: Multinational Force & Observers Medal
Denotes: Total number of awards

37a. Numeral 2 Block, Bronze

Services: Army
Worn on: NCO Professional Development Ribbon
Denotes: Level of prof. training achved ("Basic")

37b. Numeral "3", Block, Bronze

Services: Army
Worn on: NCO Professional Development Ribbon
Denotes: Level of professional training achieved ("Advanced")

37c. Numeral "4", Block, Bronze

Services: Army
Worn on: NCO Professional Development Ribbon
Denotes: Level of professional training achieved ("Senior")

37d. Numeral "5", Block, Bronze
Services: Army
Worn on: NCO Professional Development Ribbon
Denotes: Completion of Sergeants-Major Academy (Obsolete)

38. Numeral, Block, Gold

Services: Navy, Marine Corps
Worn on: Air Medal
Denotes: Total number of individual awards

39. Numeral, Scroll, Bronze
Services: Marine Corps
Worn on: Marine Corps Good Conduct and Expeditionary Medals
Denotes: Number of awards (Obsolete)

40. Numeral, Scroll, Bronze

Services: Navy
Worn on: World War II Campaign Medals
Denotes: Number of battle clasps earned (Obsolete)

41. Oak Leaf Cluster, Bronze

Services: Army, Air Force
Worn on: Personal Decorations
Denotes: One (1) additional award

42. Oak Leaf Cluster, Bronze

Services: Army, Air Force
Worn on: Unit Awards
Denotes: One (1) additional award

43. Oak Leaf Cluster, Bronze

Services: Air Force
Worn on: Service and Reserve Awards
Denotes: One (1) additional award

44. Oak Leaf Cluster, Bronze

Services: Army
Worn on: Reserve Components Achievement Medal
Denotes: One (1) additional award

45. Oak Leaf Cluster, Bronze

Services: All
Worn on: Joint Service Decorations and Joint Meritorious Unit Award
Denotes: One (1) additional award

46. Oak Leaf Cluster, Bronze

Services: Air Force
Worn on: Recognition Awards
Denotes: One (1) additional award

47. Oak Leaf Cluster, Bronze

Services: Army
Worn on: National Defense Service Medal
Denotes: One (1) additional award (Obsolete)

48. Oak Leaf Cluster, Silver

Services: Army, Air Force
Worn on: Personal Decorations
Denotes: Five (5) additional awards

49. Oak Leaf Cluster, Silver

Services: Army, Air Force
Worn on: Unit Awards
Denotes: Five (5) additional awards

Armed Forces Ribbon Devices

50. Oak Leaf Cluster, Silver

Services: Air Force
Worn on: Service and Reserve Awards
Denotes: Five (5) additional awards

51. Oak Leaf Cluster, Silver

Services: All
Worn on: Joint Service decorations and Joint Meritorious Unit Award
Denotes: Five (5) additional awards

52. Oak Leaf Cluster, Silver

Services: Air Force
Worn on: Recognition Awards
Denotes: Five (5) additional awards

53. Palm, Bronze

Services: All (Except Army)
Worn on: Vietnam Gallantry Cross Unit Citation
Denotes: No significance, worn upon initial issue

54. Palm, Bronze

Services: All
Worn on: Vietnam Civil Actions Unit Citation
Denotes: No significance, worn upon initial issue

55. Palm, Bronze

Services: Army
Worn on: Vietnam Gallantry Cross Unit Citation
Denotes: Level of Award ("Cited before the Army")

56. Palm & Swords Device, Gold

Services: All
Worn on: Kuwait Liberation Medal (Saudi Arabia)
Denotes: No significance, worn upon initial issue

57. Pistol, M1911A1, Bronze

Services: Coast Guard
Worn on: Pistol Marksmanship Ribbon
Denotes: Recipient of Pistol Shot Excellence in Competition Badge (Bronze)

58. Pistol, M1911A1, Silver

Services: Coast Guard
Worn on: Pistol Marksmanship Ribbon
Denotes: Recipient of Pistol Shot Excellence in Competition Badge (Silver)

59. Rifle, M-14, Bronze
Services: Coast Guard
Worn on: Rifle Marksmanship Ribbon
Denotes: Recipient of Rifleman Excellence in Competition Badge (Bronze)

60. Rifle, M-14, Silver

Services: Coast Guard
Worn on: Rifle Marksmanship Ribbon
Denotes: Recipient of Rifleman Excellence in Competition Badge (Silver)

61. Seahorse, Silver

Services: Merchant Marine
Worn on: Gallant Ship Citation Bar
Denotes: No significance, worn upon initial issue

62. Star 3/16" dia., Blue

Services: Navy, Marine Corps
Worn on: Navy Presidential Unit Citation
Denotes: Initial and subsequent awards (Obsolete)

63. Star 3/16" dia., Bronze

Services: All
Worn on: Campaign awards since World War II
Denotes: Battle participation (one star per major engagement)

64. Star 3/16" dia., Bronze
Services: All
Worn on: Expeditionary Medals
Denotes: Additional service (one star per designated expedition)

65. Star 3/16" dia., Bronze

Services: All
Worn on: Prisoner of War and Humanitarian Service Medals
Denotes: One (1) additional award

66. Star 3/16" dia., Bronze

Services: Navy, Marine Corps
Worn on: Unit Awards
Denotes: One (1) star per each additional award

67. Star 3/16" dia., Bronze

Services: All
Worn on: Service Awards
Denotes: One (1) star per each additional award

68. Star 3/16" dia., Bronze

Services: Navy
Worn on: Letter of Commendation Ribbon with Pendant
Denotes: One additional award (Obsolete)

69. Star 3/16" dia., Bronze
Services: Navy and Marine Corps
Worn on: Air Medal
Denotes: First individual award (Obsolete)

70. Star 3/16" dia., Bronze
Services: Air Force
Worn on: Outstanding Airman of the Year Award
Denotes: "One of 12" competition finalist

71. Star 3/16" dia., Bronze
Services: Air Force
Worn on: Small Arms Expert Marksmanship Ribbon
Denotes: Additional weapon qualification

72. Star 3/16" dia., Bronze

Services: All
Worn on: World War I Victory Medal
Denotes: One (1) star for each campaign clasp earned

73. Star 3/16" dia., Bronze

Services: Navy, Marine Corps, Coast Guard
Worn on: China Service Medal (1937-39)
Denotes: Additional award for service during (1945-57)

74. Star 3/16" dia., Bronze
Services: Coast Guard
Worn on: Combat Action Ribbon
Denotes: One (1) additional award

75. Star 3/16" dia., Bronze

Services: All
Worn on: American Defense Service Medal
Denotes: Overseas service prior to World War II

76. Star 3/16" dia., Bronze

Services: All
Worn on: National Defense Service Medal
Denotes: Additional awards (one star per designated period)

77. Star 3/16" dia., Bronze

Services: Coast Guard
Worn on: Joint Meritorious Unit Award
Denotes: One (1) additional award

78. Star 3/16" dia., Bronze

Services: Coast Guard
Worn on: Antarctica Service Medal
Denotes: One (1) additional award

79. Star 3/16" dia., Bronze

Services: All
Worn on: Philippine Defense and Liberation Ribbons & Medals
Denotes: Additional battle honors

Air and Space Force V, C and R Devices. See following pages.

Legend:
- 🇻 1st award Bronze Letter V
- 🇻 2nd award Silver Letter V
- 🇻 3rd award Gold Letter V
- C 1st award Bronze Letter C
- C 2nd award Silver Letter C
- C 3rd award Gold Letter C
- R 1st award Bronze Letter R
- R 2nd award Silver Letter R
- R 3rd award Gold Letter R

80. Star 3/16" dia., Bronze

Services: All (Except Army)
Worn on: Philippine Presidential Unit Citation
Denotes: Additional award

81. Star 3/16" dia., Bronze
Services: All
Worn on: United Nations and NATO mission medals
Denotes: One (1) star for each additional mission

82. Star 3/16" dia., Silver
Services: All
Worn on: Campaign awards since World War II
Denotes: Battle participation in five (5) major engagements

83. Star 3/16" dia., Silver
Services: All
Worn on: Expeditionary Medals
Denotes: Five (5) additional expeditions

84. Star 3/16" dia., Silver

Services: All
Worn on: Prisoner of War and Humanitarian Service Medals
Denotes: Five (5) additional awards

85. Star 3/16" dia., Silver
Services: Navy, Marine Corps
Worn on: Unit awards
Denotes: Five (5) additional awards

86. Star 3/16" dia., Silver
Services: All
Worn on: Service Awards
Denotes: Five (5) additional Awards

87. Star 3/16" dia., Silver
Services: Navy
Worn on: World War I Victory Medal
Denotes: Receipt of Letter of Commendation

88. Star 3/16" dia., Silver
Services: Army
Worn on: Campaign medals up to World War I
Denotes: Citation for Gallantry

89. Star 3/16" dia., Silver

Services: Coast Guard
Worn on: Joint Meritorious Unit Award
Denotes: Five (5) additional awards

90. Star 3/16" dia., Silver

Services: Navy
Worn on: Arctic Service
Denotes: First award (up to four North Star or Compass Rose Devices)

91. Star 5/16" dia., Bronze
Services: Navy, Marine Corps.
Worn on: Navy, USMC Expeditionary Medals
Denotes: One (1) additional award (Obsolete)

92. Star 5/16" dia., Bronze
Services: Navy, Marine Corps.
Worn on: Haitian Campaign Medal (1915)
Denotes: Subsequent award of the "1919-1920" Clasp

93. Star 5/16" dia., Gold
Services: Navy, Marine Corps, Coast Guard
Worn on: Personal Decorations
Denotes: One (1) additional award

94. Star 5/16" dia., Gold
Services: Coast Guard
Worn on: Unit awards
Denotes: One (1) additional award

95. Star 5/16" dia., Gold

Services: Air Force
Worn on: Combat Action Medal
Denotes: One (1) additional award

96. Star 5/16" dia., Gold
Services: Navy, Marine Corps
Worn on: Combat Action Ribbon
Denotes: One (1) additional award

97. Star 5/16" dia., Gold
Services: Coast Guard
Worn on: Joint Service Awards
Denotes: One (1) additional award (Obsolete)

98. Star 5/16" dia., Gold
Services: Coast Guard
Worn on: Lifesaving Medals
Denotes: One (1) additional award

99. Star 5/16" dia., Gold
Services: All
Worn on: Inter-American Defense Board Medal
Denotes: One (1) denotes 5 years service on IADB.

100. Star 5/16" dia., Gold
Services: Army
Worn on: Army Sea Duty Ribbon
Denotes: 10th (final) award

101. Star 5/16" dia., Silver
Services: Navy, Marine Corps, Coast Guard
Worn on: Personal Decorations
Denotes: Five (5) additional awards

102. Star 5/16" dia., Silver
Services: Coast Guard
Worn on: Unit Awards
Denotes: Five (5) additional awards

103. Letter N, Bronze
Services: Air & Space
Worn on: Nuclear Deterrence Opns Service Awards
Denotes: Nuclear Weapons Service

104. Letter V, Bronze, Silver, Gold
🇻 🇻 🇻
Services: Air & Space
Worn on: Select Valor Awards
Denotes: Number of Valor Awards. See page 20 for details.

105. Number, Bronze

Services: All
Worn on: DOD Decorations in lieu of silver oak leaf
Denotes: Number of awards

108. Target, Pistol, Gold
Services: Coast Guard
Worn on: Pistol Marksmanship Ribbon
Denotes: Recipient of Distinguished Pistol Shot Badge

109. Target, Rifle, Gold
Services: Coast Guard
Worn on: Rifle Marksmanship Ribbon
Denotes: Recipient of Distinguished Marksman Badge

110. Letter C, Bronze
Services: New for all
Worn on: Personal decorations
Denote: Award was earned in a combat setting

111. Letter R, Bronze
Services: New for All
Worn on: Personal decorations
Denotes: Recognize remote combat action.

Placement of the Letter "V" on the Ribbon

No. of Awards	Army & Old USAF V Device	Navy	Marine Corps	New Air & Space Force V Device	Coast Guard
1	V	V	V	V	V
2	V 🍂	★ V	★ V	V	★ V
3	V 🍂🍂	★ V ★	★ V ★	V	★ V ★
4	V 🍂🍂🍂	★★ V ★	★★ V ★	⊻	★★ V ★
5	SEE NOTE 1	★★ V ★★	★★ V ★★	⊻	★★ V ★★
6	V 🍂	★ V	★ V	⊻	★ V
7	V 🍂🍂	★ V ★	★ V ★	⊻ V	★ V ★
8	V 🍂🍂🍂	★★ V ★	★★ V ★	⊻ V	★★ V ★

Legend: Sea Services
- ★ = 5/16" Gold Star
- ☆ = 5/16" Silver Star
- V = Bronze Letter V
- V = Gold Letter V

Legend: Army & Old USAF
- V = Bronze Letter V
- 🍂 = Silver Oak Leaf Cluster
- 🍂 = Bronze Oak Leaf Cluster

Legend: Air and Space Force
- V = 1st award Bronze Letter V
- V = 2nd award Silver Letter V
- V = 3rd award Gold Letter V

Legend: Air and Space Force
- ⊻ = 4th award Bronze w/ wreath
- ⊻ = 5th award Silver w/ wreath
- ⊻ = 6th award Gold w/ wreath

Placement of Devices on the Armed Forces Reserve Medal

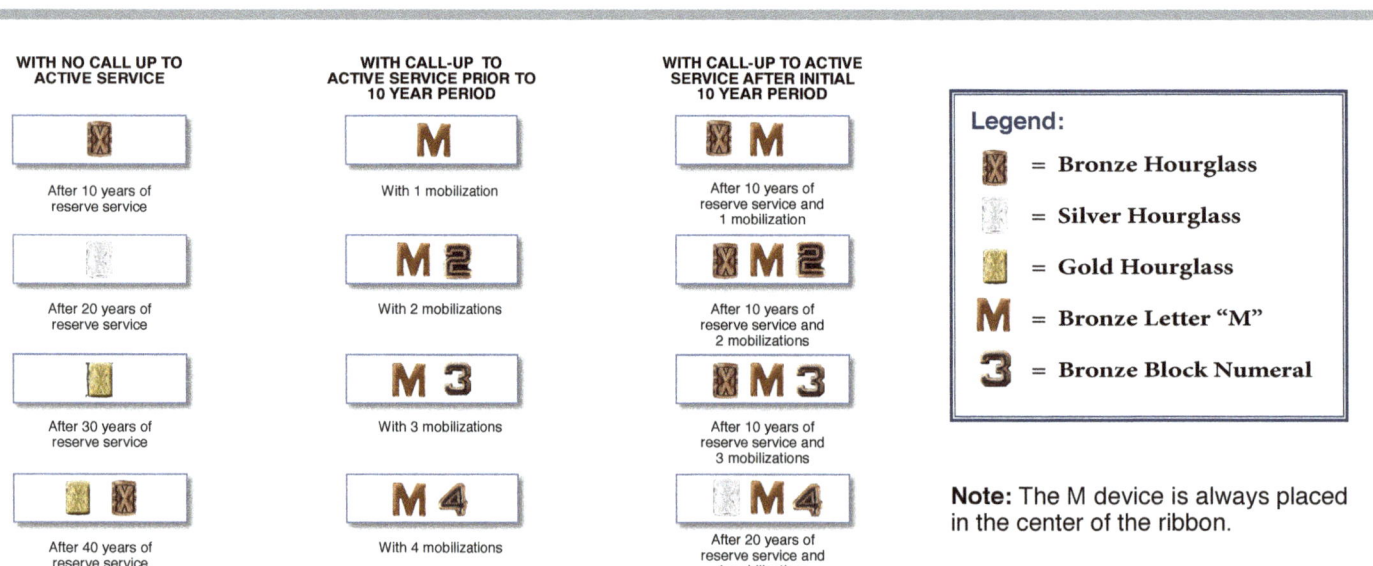

Legend:
- ⌛ = Bronze Hourglass
- ⌛ = Silver Hourglass
- ⌛ = Gold Hourglass
- M = Bronze Letter "M"
- 3 = Bronze Block Numeral

Note: The M device is always placed in the center of the ribbon.

Placement of Silver & Gold Stars and Bronze & Silver Oak Leaf Devices on Ribbons

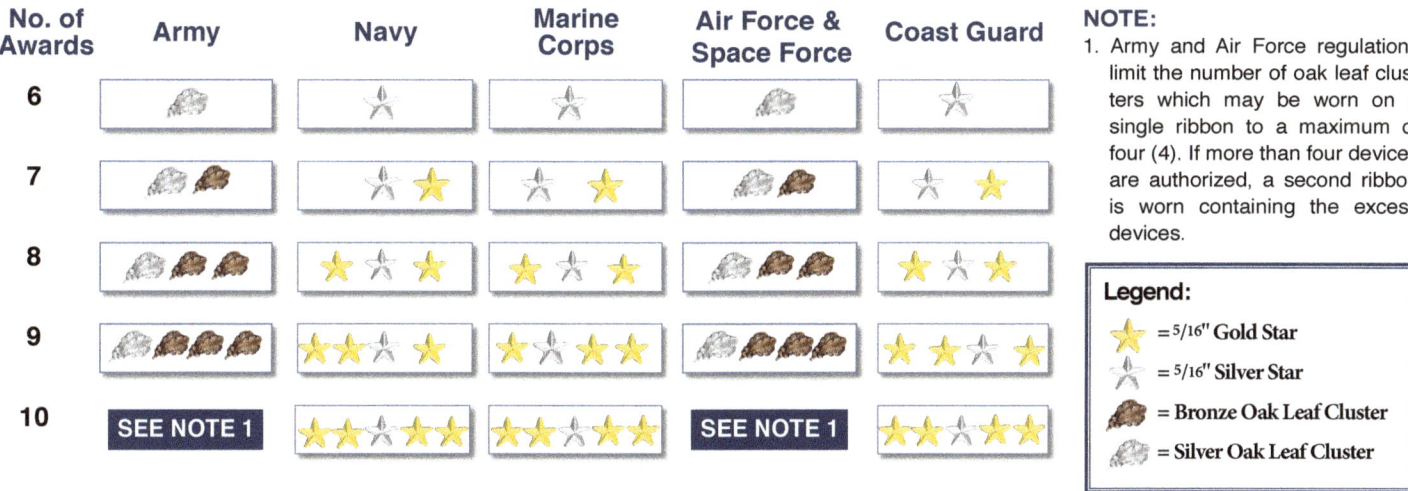

NOTE:
1. Army and Air Force regulations limit the number of oak leaf clusters which may be worn on a single ribbon to a maximum of four (4). If more than four devices are authorized, a second ribbon is worn containing the excess devices.

Legend:
- ★ = 5/16" Gold Star
- ☆ = 5/16" Silver Star
- 🍂 = Bronze Oak Leaf Cluster
- 🍃 = Silver Oak Leaf Cluster

Placement of Oak Leaf Cluster Devices on Army & DOD Ribbons

NOTES:
1. Army and Air Force regulations limit the number of devices which may be worn on a single ribbon to a maximum of four (4). If more than four devices are authorized, a second ribbon is worn containing the excess devices.
2. Joint Service and DOD awards now are limited to 4 total devices so numerals are used to replace multiple oak leaf clusters. Silver OLCs are not authorized to be worn on the same decoration or award that has received a V,C and R Devices, so Numerals are used to replace silver OLCs. See page 23 for details.

No. of Awards	All Services	No. of Awards	
1		6	🍃
2	🍂	7	🍃🍂
3	🍂🍂	8	🍃🍂🍂
4	🍂🍂🍂	9	🍃🍂🍂🍂
5	🍂🍂🍂🍂	10	SEE NOTE 2

Legend:
- 🍂 = Bronze Oak Leaf Cluster
- 🍃 = Silver Oak Leaf Cluster

Device Usage on the Navy Air Medal

Navy and Marine Corps (Individual Awards)

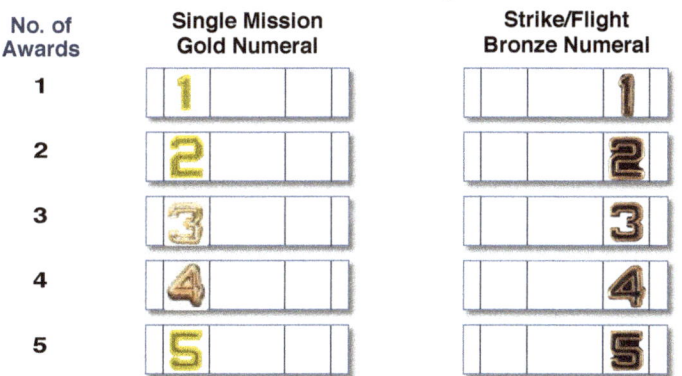

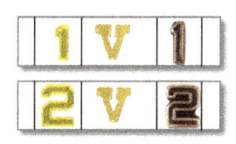

Flights are combat sorties that do not encounter enemy opposition.

Since 5 April, 1974, the Combat "V" may be authorized for awards for heroism or meritorious action in conflict with an armed enemy.

Ribbon devices (1989–2006)
Between 22 November, 1989, and 27 September, 2006, 3/16 inch bronze stars, 5/16 inch gold stars, and 5/16 inch silver stars denoted the number of "Individual" Air Medals. A bronze star denoted a first award. Gold stars were used for the second through the fifth awards with Silver stars used for five gold stars. For "Individual" Air Medals, the Combat "V" could be authorized.

Bronze Strike/Flight numerals denoted the number of Strike/Flight awards authorized for operations in hostile or disputed territory and count the total number of Strikes (operations that faced enemy opposition) and Flights (operations that did not encounter enemy opposition) added together.

Air Medal Device Arrangements. As of 27 September, 2006, gold Numeral devices are used to denote the number of "Individual" Air Medals. Bronze Strike/Flight numerals denote the total number of Strike/Flight awards. Strikes are combat sorties that do encounter enemy opposition.

Placement Campaign Stars on the Ribbon

No. of Campaigns	All Service	No. of Campaigns	Army & Air & Space Force	Navy	Marine Corps	Coast Guard
1	★	5	✦	✦	✦	✦
2	★★	6	✦ ★	✦ ★	✦ ★	✦ ★
3	★★★	7	✦ ★★	★★✦	★✦★	★✦★
4	★★★★	8	✦★★★	★★✦★	★✦★★	★★✦★
5	✦	9	SEE NOTE 1	★★✦★★	★★✦★★	★★✦★★

NOTE:
1. Army and Air Force regulations limit the number of devices which may be worn on a single ribbon to a maximum of four. If more than four devices are authorized, a second ribbon is worn containing the excess devices.
2. Campaign stars are often referred to as "Battle Stars".

Arrowhead, Bronze
In the Army the Bronze Arrowhead is awarded for Combat assault or invasion and always goes to the right of Campaign Stars.

FMF Device, Bronze
The FMF is worn by Naval combat personnel with Marine Corps units and always goes in the center of the ribbon.

Legend:
★ = 3/16" Bronze Star
✦ = 3/16" Silver Star

Placement of the C Combat & R Remote Device on the Ribbon

No. of Awards	Army C Device	Navy C Device	USMC C Device	New Air & Space Force C Device	USCG C Device
1	C	C	C	C	C
2	C 🍃	★C	★C	C	★C
3	C 🍃🍃	★C★	★C★	C	★C★
4	C 🍃🍃🍃	★★C★	★★C★	❂	★★C★
5	SEE NOTE 1	★★C★★	★★C★★	❂	★★C★★

No. of Awards	Army R Device	Navy R Device	USMC R Device	New Air & Space Force R Device	USCG R Device
1	R	R	R	R	R
2	R 🍃	★R	★R	R	★R
3	R 🍃🍃	★R★	★R★	R	★R★
4	R 🍃🍃🍃	★★R★	★★R★	❂	★★R★
5	SEE NOTE 1	★★R★★	★★R★★	❂	★★R★★

When both C and R bronze device are awarded the C goes before the R and the V before both.

| CR | VCR | CR 🍃 | ★CR |

Placement of Devices on DOD Joint Decorations and Awards

No. of Awards	With V Device	C Device	R Device	Multiple awards	Multiple Devices
1	V	C	R		V
2	V 🍂	C 🍂	R 🍂	🍂	V R
3	V 🍂🍂	C 🍂🍂	R 🍂🍂	🍂🍂	V C R
4	V 🍂🍂🍂	C 🍂🍂🍂	R 🍂🍂🍂	🍂🍂🍂	V C R 🍂
5	V 4	C 4	R 4	🍂🍂🍂🍂	V C R 2
6	V 5	C 5	R 5	⭐	V C R 3

NOTES:
1. Joint Service and DOD awards now are limited to 4 total devices so numerals are used to replace multiple oak leaf clusters.
2. Silver OLCs are not authorized to be worn on the same Decoration or Award that has received a V, C, or R Device, so numerals are used to repace silver OLCs.
3. The V Device is always worn before the C and R Devices, and the R Device is always worn after the V and C Devices.

United States Merchant Marines Decorations and Medals

The Purple Heart Medal has been approved for members of the Merchant Marine wounded in the line of duty during war time.

Bronzer Service Star denotes second and subsequent awards of a service award or participation in a campaign or operation.

Silver Service Star Indicates crew member forced to abandon ship.

Silver Seahorse Worn in Gallant Ship Citation Bar upon initial issue but has no significance.

Distinguished Service Medal		Meritorious Service Medal		Mariner's Medal	
None		None		None	
Outstanding Achievement Medal	Gallant Ship Citation Bar	Merchant Marine Combat Bar	Prisoner of War Medal
None	Silver	Silver	Bronze
Merchant Marine Defense Medal	Atlantic War Zone Medal	Pacific War Zone Medal	Mediterranean-Middle East War Zone Medal
None	None	None	None
World War II Victory Medal	Korean Service Medal	Vietnam Service Medal	Merchant Marine Expeditionary Medal
None	None	None	Bronze
Philippine Defense Medal	Philippine Liberation Medal	40th Anniversary of World War II (USSR)	50th Anniversary of World War II (Russia)
Bronze	Bronze	None	None

Service Notes on Wearing Military Ribbons

United States Army

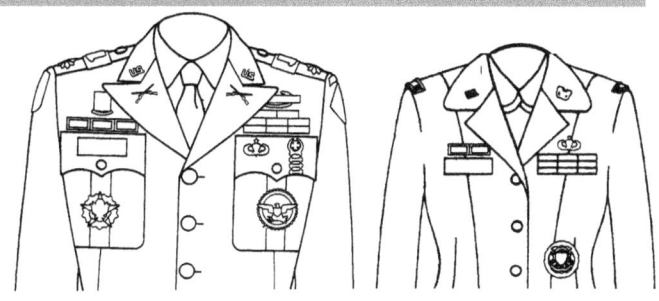

Wear of Service Ribbons — Ribbons may be worn on the Army blue and white uniform coats or shirt. The ribbons are worn in one or more rows in order of precedence with either no space or 1/8 inch between rows, no more than four ribbons to a row. The top row is centered or aligned to left edge of the row underneath, whichever looks the best. Unit awards are centered above the right breast pocket with a maximum of three per row.

United States Navy

(The Coast Guard generally follows U.S. Navy guidelines)

Wear of Service Ribbons — Wear up to 3 in a row; if more than three ribbons, wear in horizontal rows of three each. The top row contains the lesser number, centered above the row below, no spaces between ribbon rows. Rows of ribbons covered by coat lapel may contain two ribbons each and be aligned. Wear ribbons with lower edge of bottom row centered 1/4 inch above left breast and parallel to the deck.

Coast Guard members may either wear the senior three ribbons or all ribbons when they are covered by lapel by 1/3 or more. Rows can be decreased to 2 or 1 if all ribbons are worn in this situation.

United States Marine Corps

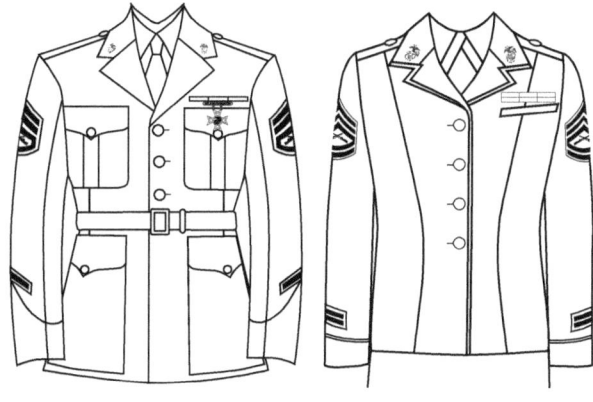

Wear of Service Ribbons — Ribbons are authorized on Marine dress "B", dress "A" or shirts when prescribed as an outer garment. They are normally worn in rows of 3 or rows of 4 when displaying a large number of awards. If the lapel conceals any ribbons, they may be placed in successively decreasing rows, i.e., 4, 3, 2, 1. All aligned vertically on center, except if the top row can be altered to present the neatest appearance. Ribbon rows may be spaced 1/8 inch apart or together. Ribbon bars are centered 1/8 inch above the upper left pocket. When marksmanship badges are worn, the ribbon bars are 1/8 inch above them.

United States Air Force

Wear of Service Ribbons — Ribbons may be worn on service dress and blue shirt. Ribbons are normally worn in rows of three with the bottom bar centered and resting on the top edge of the pocket. Ribbons may be worn four-in-a-row with the left edge of the ribbons aligned with the left edge of the pocket to keep the lapel from covering ribbons. There is no space between rows of ribbons. Current regulations stipulate that members may choose which ribbons to wear, if any.

Ribbon display shown on older USAF dress blue uniform.

Other Great Medals and Insignia Books All Available at
WWW.MOAPress.com
or on Amazon

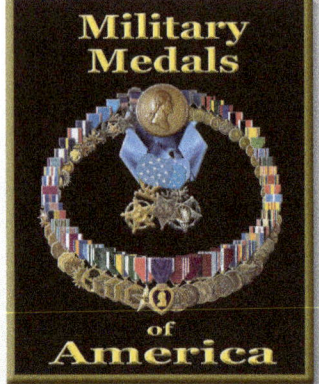

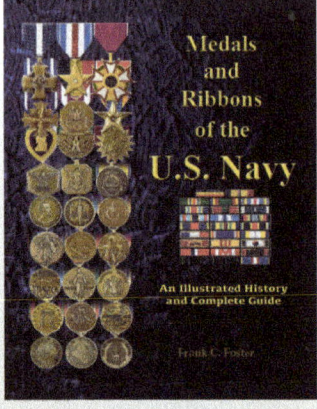

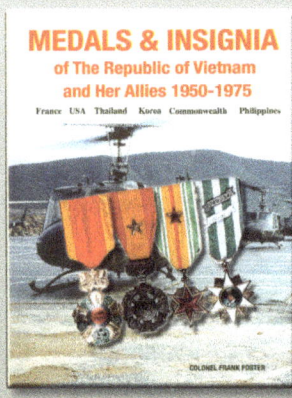
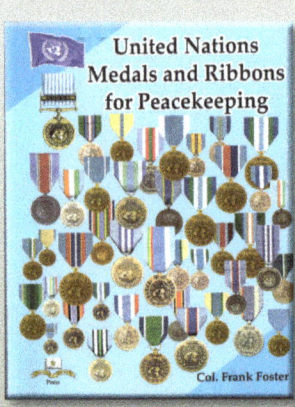
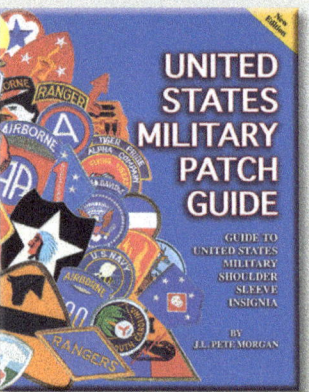

America's Best Medal and Ribbon Wear Guides All Available at
WWW.MOAPress.com
or on Amazon

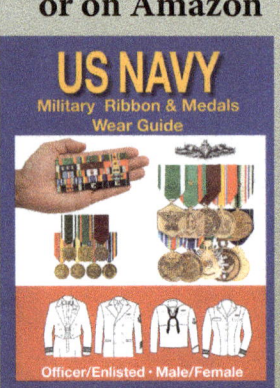

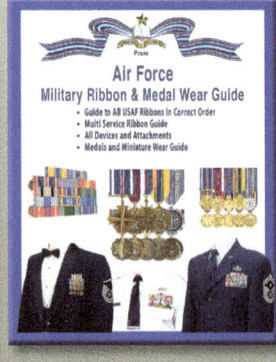

ISBN - 978-1-884452-64-2

www.ingramcontent.com/pod-product-compliance
Lightning Source LLC
Chambersburg PA
CBHW051351110526
44591CB00025B/2975